D1351833

Greene on Capri

GREENE *on* CAPRI

A Memoir

SHIRLEY HAZZARD

A *Virago* Book

Published by Virago Press 2000

Published by arrangement with Farrar, Straus and Giroux LLC,
19 Union Square West, New York, NY, 10003, USA

Copyright © Shirley Hazzard 2000

The moral right of the author has been asserted

A CIP catalogue record for this book
is available from the British Library

ISBN 1 86049 799 3

Printed and bound in Great Britain by Clays Ltd, St Ives plc

Virago Press
A Division of
Little, Brown and Company (UK)
Brettenham House
Lancaster Place
London WC2E 7EN

For F. S.,

who shared it all

Graham Greene, Capri, c. 1949

Greene on Capri

O N A DECEMBER MORNING of the late 1960s, I was sitting by the windows of the Gran Caffè in the piazzetta of Capri, doing the crossword in *The Times*. The weather was wet, as it had been for days, and the looming rock face of the Monte Solaro dark with rain. High seas, and some consequent suspension of the Naples ferry, had interrupted deliveries from the mainland; and the newspaper freshly arrived from London was several days old. In the café, the few other tables were unoccupied. An occasional waterlogged Caprese—workman or shopkeeper—came to take coffee at the counter. There was steam from wet wool and espresso; a clink and clatter of small cups and spoons; an exchange of words in dialect. It was near noon.

Two tall figures under umbrellas appeared in the empty square and loped across to the café: a pair of Englishmen wearing raincoats, and one—the elder—with a black beret. The man with the beret was Graham Greene. I recognised him—as one would; and also because I had seen him in the past on Capri, at the restaurant Gemma near the piazza, where he dined at a corner table with his companion, and great love of the postwar decade, Catherine Walston. That was in the late 1950s, when I used to visit Naples and Capri from Siena, where I then spent part of the year. One knew that Greene had a house in the town of Anacapri, in the upper portion of the island, which he had visited faithfully if sporadically for many years.

On that damp December morning, Greene and his dark-haired friend came into the Gran Caffè, hung their coats, and sat down at the next tiny table to mine. I went on with my puzzle; but it was impossible not to overhear the conversation of my neighbours— or, at any rate, not to hear one side of it. Graham Greene certainly did not have a loud voice, but his speech was incisive, with distinctive inflections, and his voice was lowered only in asides or to make confidences. It was an individual voice, developed before the great British flattening, when one's manner of speaking might, beyond any affectation of class, become personal speech: one's own expressive instrument casting its spell in conversation. I would in any case have noticed what he was saying, because he began to quote from a poem by Robert Browning called "The Lost Mistress." The poem opens:

All's over then: does truth sound bitter . . .

but the passage that especially interested Greene comes later:

Tomorrow we meet the same, then, dearest?
May I take your hand in mine?
Mere friends are we—well, friends the merest
Keep much that I resign . . .

He went on to quote the poem's concluding verse, but could not recall the last line. The lines he recited, and repeated, are

Yet I will but say what mere friends say,
Or only a thought stronger;
I will hold your hand but as long as all may—

And then he could not remember the very end. He recurred to this several times, trying to draw it up from his memory, but did not manage it.

When I had finished my coffee and my puzzle, and had paid, and had taken my raincoat and umbrella from the dank stand, I said, "The line is

"Or so very little longer."

I went away at once, back under the rain to the Hotel San Felice—where we used to stay on visits to Capri until, soon after that December trip, we rented, in an old house, a simple flat that became our Capri perch for the next quarter-century. Francis—my husband, Francis Steegmuller—was waiting for me. And of course I told the story, which had already become a story. Francis had met Greene years earlier, in New York, when Graham, with his wife Vivien, was on a postwar trip to America of which he retained few good impressions. Later, Francis and Graham had briefly corresponded. The morning's encounter on Capri seemed to me, and seems still, like an incident from a novel: from a real novel, a good novel, an old novel. And I imagine that it appeared so to Graham also.

That evening, as we arrived at our fireside table in the inner room at Gemma's restaurant, Graham, with his friend Michael Richey, stood up to greet us. We dined together. And so began our years of seeing Greene on Capri.

A day or so later, Graham asked us to lunch at his house in Anacapri. In rather better weather we took the bus up the vertiginous road of the Monte Solaro, the island's presiding dolomitic mountain. Getting out in Piazza Caprile—a farthermost enclave of the little town of Anacapri, which runs along a ridge of the Solaro slope—we walked the couple of hundred yards to Graham's gate. Il Rosaio, as the house is called, sharing its name with an adjacent property, dates in present form from about 1922. It belongs to a period when the ancient rustic architecture of Capri, compact, domed, and curved, was taken up by certain of the island's more worldly residents—and in particular by an entrepreneurial mentor of Capri, Edwin Cerio—as a basis for constructing charming houses: white, but not starkly so; well made but never massive; not luxurious, but comfortable, and appropriate to climate and surroundings. A score or more of these houses, each different but linked in style, are scattered through the island, most of them still in private hands. The danger of such emulative architecture—that it may seem coy, or toy—has long since been exorcised by the Capri climate, which, through seasonal alternations of scorching and soaking, weathers any tactful, durable structure into authenticity. The island's prolific growth of flowering plants, shrubs, and vines does the rest.

The wrought-iron gate of the Rosaio is set into the arch of a high white wall and provided with a bell and bellpull. You walk into a secluded garden reminiscent of Greece or North Africa, and characteristic, even today, of many Capri dwellings where the island's history of "Saracen" assaults by sea, and its once imperative climatic needs, linger in structural patterns common to all the Mediterranean. Intersecting paths paved with old rosy bricks lead, as in a childhood dream, to the obscure front door. The slight suggestion of a maze would have attracted the author of *Ways of Escape*. The house is small, its ground floor having four rooms and the upper storey consisting only of a single ledge-like space. (At a later time, Graham had a portion of the roof fitted up as a sheltered terrace that looks down the island's long western slope to the sea and over to the cone of Ischia on the horizon, providing vermilion views of extravagant sunsets.) The entire space of the property—imaginatively expanded, by censorious writers on Greene, into a site of sybaritic luxury—is that of a suburban English cottage with its pleasant plot of ground. The core of that particular criticism may be that the Rosaio is not suburban: it is on Capri.

Pine cones and short logs were burning in the convex fireplace of the little living room where we had drinks with Graham and his houseguest, Michael Richey. Richey, a writer, sculptor, graphic artist, lone long-distance sailor, and, for many years, Director of the Royal Institute of Navigation, had met Graham in London in 1940. With a hiatus for war service, the friendship had been maintained ever since. Talk started up at once, favoured by the intimacy and simplicity of the setting. There were books, a few small pictures ("That one is by a former girlfriend"), a Neapolitan eighteenth-century crèche figure of the Madonna under its bell jar; the whole—easy, agreeable, cosy without clutter.

The room's high ceiling culminates in a miniature dome, or lantern, of paned glass giving extra light on dark days. The floor is of old white tiles set with tiled borders of green leaves and yellow flowers. Tiles of such quality and durability, with a depth of as much as two inches, have been a feature of Neapolitan pavements and decoration for centuries—overflowing, in the eighteenth century, into entire polychrome scenes in churches, cloisters, and palaces of the region. Locally known as *le riggiole,* they are individually fired, and can be reproduced, and laid, these days, only at high expense. Their beauty is enhanced by the tactile purity of a glaze luminous yet livable that—as in the case of Graham's white floors—suggests, by some fugitive tinge of rose, the underlying terracotta.

In a dining room, where winter light came through a set of small, high windows, our lunch of pasta and a fowl was served by Carmelina, who, with her husband, Aniello, and their family, cared for Graham on his visits and attended throughout the year to the house and garden. Short and staunch, with a coloured kerchief knotted over her coiled grey hair and an ample apron on her dark dress, Carmelina was a picture of the hardworking, good-humoured Caprese *massaia* of her day: firm women, not without irony, who lived close to the land and the seasons, to weather, crops, and vines; to the daily narrative of the parish and the community; and, most deeply, to the ties of blood.

Many such women seldom left the island, even for a day's trip to Naples, twenty miles away. Theirs was the last generation of which that would be true.

Our hours went quickly, in talk and laughter. We drank a good amount of Anacapri's genuine light red wine, already becoming rare. There was pleasure, self-evidently shared, and some mild excitement in the oddity of that winter meeting on a Mediterranean rock: a brief adventure quickened by what Graham valued most, the unexpected.

Graham then was in his mid-sixties; Francis, two years younger; Michael Richey, late forties. I was in my thirties. Graham and Michael were both Catholics, Graham having converted at the time of his youthful marriage. (Years later, after Graham's death, Michael wrote to me: "One bond—if it's not too high-falutin' a concept— was Catholicism; it would not have been the same without that.") Francis, raised in a Catholic family, had withdrawn from the Church in early youth. I had grown up a perfunctory Anglican. We were, all four, writers and readers in a world where the expressive word, spoken or written, still seemed paramount—beneficiaries of what John Bayley once called "the inevitable solace that right language brings." We were all, in varying degrees, sociable yet solitary.

Graham's receding hair was grey, and would soon be white. His slightly stooping walk and posture were the mark less of the ageing writer than of the English schoolboy: into his last years, one would still perceive the gangling, narrow-shouldered, self-communing youth. His only "exercise" was walking—and he had walked, in his time, across countries and continents—but his body had the loose agility that derives from a lifelong sense of being thin, lanky, alert, and tall. His hands were at once notable: fine, strong, energised; subtle, but entirely masculine—the fingers flatly attenuated, the palms somewhat afflicted by what I imagine was Dupuytren's contracture, a condition in which a strap of thickened tissue progressively constricts the flesh. Those hands, vibrant even when still, proposed the entire prehensive faculty. At table, Graham habitually propped his chin or cheek on his left hand, as one might assume he did while working—not in a tapered, reflective, "Georgian" pose, but with tight fist, the knuckles edging bone. Or his fingers were lightly splayed on the tablecloth, like spokes of a half-closed fan. His occasional gestures had nothing to do with the disarray of "body language." They were the gestures of a succinctly articulate man: slight, sparing, controlled, idiosyncratic; confined, except for a thin shrug, to the hands and concentrated in the fingertips. Hands, like body, conveyed acuity. There was restraint, but not repose.

His presence was immediate and interesting, with its emanation of expectancy and experience. His face was charged with feelings unhallowed and unmellowed, and lit by the blue, extraordinary eyes.

Graham Greene's eyes have been much described, and they were, in later years, occasionally photographed. They were part of his magnetism, and he knew it; but their power was not feigned. For his friend, the Italian writer Mario Soldati, Graham had "blue fire in his eyes, the eyes of a demon." Soldati told Greene's biographer Norman Sherry that Graham

> had what I would call a hurt, offended face, metaphorically bruised by events, the expression, not continuously but every once in a while, of an angry and hurt face even when something small went wrong . . . There was something unearthly in those eyes.

At the time of our meeting, and through most of his life, Graham was a good-looking man—personable, and used to being attractive to women. In physiognomy and bearing he was clearly an Englishman of his era, but his looks belonged to no convention and fluctuated with mood. In his sixties, the short upper lip of sensitive youth was lengthening and toughening, the mouth pursing, the lower face growing jowly, the cheeks and nose pinkly veined from a past of serious drinking. Full face, the eyes were rounded, the lower lids drooping on a reddish rim. (Himself the keenest Greene-watcher of all, he sometimes endowed his fictional characters with

those same eyes: "The brandy [affected] even the physical appearance of his eye-balls. It was as if the little blood-cells had been waiting under the white membrane to burst at once like buds.") The
blue glassy stare, often challenging or antagonistic, was never
veiled. In the demon rages, the eyes would glare out, accusatory,
engorged with fluid resentment. From under frizzy white brows,
the eyesockets appeared then to deepen, the eyeballs to protrude
with a playground will to hurt, humiliate, ridicule. At those awful
moments, Graham looked for all the world like Thomas Mitchell
playing Scarlett's demented father.

His humours were conveyed intensely through the eyes—not
only the lightning anger, but curiosity, too, and the readiness for
amusement, engagement, event; as well as the literary intelligence
in its originality and rigour, its extraordinary range and freedom.
There was much conviction, some exasperated courage; there could
be recognition, candour, reasonableness, and a degree of passing
goodwill. But not, in my experience, tenderness: that is, there was
no self-forgetful surrender—whether to affection or to the vulnerable shades of trust or remorse; still less, to any enduring state of
happiness. The avowed "sliver of ice in the heart" could at times
loom forth as, merely, the tip of an iceberg,

Graham had many pleasures and, perhaps, even in later years,
some euphoric moments. But enjoyment was transitory and not, to
him, a necessity: a disposition, deeply attributable to temperament,
which should also be referred to his background and generation. As
with other Englishmen of his age—who had become adolescent
during the slaughter of the 1914–18 war, and adult with the Great
Depression—pleasure could not be an assumption and was not
a goal; whereas suffering was a constant, and almost a code of

honour. Suffering was the attestable key to imaginative existence. "Happiness" had an element of inanity, verified by Greene in life and in his fiction: "Point me out the happy man and I will point you out either egotism, selfishness, evil—or else an absolute ignorance."

(Flaubert, in a letter of 1846, also felt that "to be stupid, selfish, and have good health are three requirements for happiness, though if stupidity is lacking, all is lost." Acknowledging the possibility of a higher form of happiness, achieved incidentally in the exercise of deeper capacities, Flaubert felt that, in his own case, that, too, would remain phantasmal.)

One of Graham's rare contemporary admirations, Padre Pio—a south Italian village priest said to be afflicted with the stigmata— asserted that "suffering is the test and testimony of love." In Greene, however, I think that suffering was a requirement of consciousness itself: an agitation of spirit providing some defence against the dreaded *accidie.* "I feel discomfort, therefore I am alive"—so writes the exhausted protagonist of Graham's *A Burnt-Out Case* in the opening sentence of that novel.

The elation of sexual passion itself is repeatedly portrayed, by Graham, as frantic or despairing. Here is the narrator of *The Comedians* making love: "I flung myself into pleasure like a suicide on to a pavement."

In Mario Soldati's novel *The Capri Letters,* the central character observes that human beings need unhappiness at least as much as they need happiness. (*Almeno* is mistranslated—surprisingly, by Archibald Colquhoun—in the English language edition of that book as "almost as much," as if shirking the issue.) Soldati assigns this thoroughly European view to his American protagonist. I would say that Graham Greene needed disquiet in many forms, not least in his pleasures.

Graham's hostility to the American "way of life" was exacerbated by what he considered a contemptible national quest for the Grail of happiness—the pursuit itself, as he felt, unworthily enshrined as an ideal in the nation's founding Declaration, with the goal soon defined as materialism and indulgence. When we once spoke of Thomas Hardy's lines explaining the poet's refusal, on grounds of his own fateful view of existence, of an invitation to visit the United States—

> *My ardours for emprize nigh lost*
> *Since Life has bared its bones to me,*
> *I shrink to seek a modern coast*
> *Whose riper times have yet to be;*
> *Where the new regions claim them free*
> *From that long drip of human tears*
> *Which peoples old in tragedy*
> *Have left upon the centuried years . . .*

—Graham said that he had no doubt that tears in plenty were shed in America; but that, without the shared pathos of acknowledged pain, they were shed in bafflement and felt as failure. Bringing to mind a theme of *The Quiet American,* he held that a policy of good cheer was often a repudiation of feeling: a licence for indifference or ruthlessness.

I agreed. "Pollyanna is a cruel goddess."

Francis said, "An inartistic one, too."

That longing for "peace," which Graham invoked throughout his life, in published and in private writings, seemed, on the other hand, a fantasy of transfiguration. Anyone who knew him—and he knew himself best of all—was aware that peace was the last thing he desired. It was literally the last thing, synonymous—as often in his fiction—with death. (In *The Quiet American,* we are told that Phuong, the narrator's Vietnamese mistress, sometimes "seemed invisible like peace"—a peace in that instance embodied in the doll-like passivity of a discreet servant.) Graham's recurring suicidal impulse—that flirting with fatality in adolescence and in his terrible prewar journeys, and in later expeditions to battle zones around the world—was countered or complemented by a defiant entanglement with life; and by a nearly nineteenth-century energy of intention that enabled him to come through, and to write.

On our first afternoon at the Rosaio, pleasure held firm. Graham related the context of his quotation from Browning that had brought us together. He and Michael Richey had been to Mass in Santo Stefano, the handsome baroque church that stands as if on a platform overlooking the small central piazza of Capri, above a flight of steps, its façade averted from the cloister-like quadrangle of boutiques and cafés that was once sacred ground. (One flank of the church forms a wall of the square, providing—in a Caprese mélange of sacred, pagan, profane, and commercial—premises for a pleasant café named the Bar Tiberio, whose interior has been delved out of the Santo Stefano crypt.) In the late 1960s, the revisions of the Roman Catholic liturgy were still sufficiently recent for the "new Mass" to be a subject of discussion. Graham told us that, as he and Michael left the church for the Gran Caffè, he had suggested that the innovation of the handclasp that precedes Communion, when members of the congregation greet their neighbours in the pew, might afford an agreeable sensation "if one stationed oneself next to a pretty girl." Hence—"*I will hold your hand but as long as all may*" . . .

That day, names and themes came up that would reappear in Graham's conversation: Henry James, a lifelong and at that time unqualified enthusiasm; Conrad, of course; Francis Parkman, unforeseen but not surprising; Robert Louis Stevenson, related to Graham through maternal cousinage and, more intimately, through literary affinity; Arthur Hugh Clough, sceptical poet at odds with the Victorian age and underrated ever since. (F. and I praised Clough's long epistolary "Italian" poem, "Amours de Voyage," which Graham had not read.) There was Evelyn Waugh, a formidable friend with whom Graham shared chronology, an upbringing in the British professional class, a respect for the English language, a gift for fiction nurtured in the literary Britain of their time, and a Catholic conversion. Greene and Waugh were alike, also, in some dire aspects of temper, in the force of an angry blue stare, and in an intermittent compulsion to wreak social and emotional havoc.

We found associations in common: with Harold Acton ("Harold and I were cat and dog at Oxford. Even then I had a regard for him—he was generous and fearless. But it was later that we became friends"); with Rupert Hart-Davis, who had come to Graham's aid in their early days as writers; with Peter Quennell, whom Graham had known since schooldays but with whom his relations were, at that moment, "a bit shaky"; with Elizabeth Bowen: "A very old friend. I like her books, too, except for that one about the spy." (*The Heat of the Day* remains a favourite of mine.) Graham discovered that Francis and I had met through Muriel Spark: "I don't know her but I admire her writing." He did not say that—as I knew from Muriel—he had regularly and privately sent money to help her survive her lean first years of writing fiction, the cheques arriving each month with, in Muriel's words, "a few bottles of red wine to take the edge off cold charity." Greene did similar good by stealth, over many years, for other needy writers—among them the Indian novelist R. K. Narayan, to whom he gave inestimable material and professional help. One gradually learned, through chance testimony, of financial and practical aid to friends down on their luck, and to charitable concerns where he felt interest and saw authenticity.

Frugality, by contrast, was another note that would recur. When we admired the Rosaio, Graham told us that he had bought the house in 1948 for, as I recall, about four thousand pounds: "Completely equipped, too—dishes, pots, sheets, blankets, all included." Even in those years, it was an outstanding bargain for a modest property that today, with the crazed appreciation of Capri real estate, might fetch a million dollars. Thereafter, Graham was to relate this coup to us, together with its pots and pans, whenever the charm of his house was mentioned. In the island's older houses such as his, humidity is invincible; and in winter, ceramic floors, high ceilings, and thick walls intensify the chill. On that December afternoon, the fireplace was faintly supplemented by central

heating, the host's complaints about the cost of heating fuel—
"I don't mind cold, for myself"—being borne with equanimity
by his houseguest, whose history of solitary transatlantic cross-
ings under sail did not, in fact, point to molly-coddling. In later
years we became accustomed to those ritual invocations of economy—to Graham's consulting his watch as we lingered over dinner at Gemma: "Mustn't miss the last bus. It would mean taking
a taxi."

Most obviously, it was a means of countering assumptions
about his wealth. But one came to understand that the manner-
isms of a labyrinthine man were almost always consciously deployed—and not merely to disconcert, although that motive was
seldom absent. To have asked, Why should you care?—about
the price of heating oil, the fare of the taxi, the ticket for the
hydrofoil—would have been rude. It would also have involved
falling into a trap prepared by Graham's insistence on a need for
thrift: he would have provoked an impertinence that could be
resented. (Graham regularly invited you to step on a rug, which
he would then pull out from under.) As it was, a strain of illogic
underlay such assertions—acceded to, for the sake of calm; but
unresolved.

Born in 1904 into a well-to-do family, Graham had, long before
our meeting on Capri, become rich through his prolific writings of
novels, stories, memoirs, articles, essays, plays, and screenplays. In
his twenties and thirties, however, he had suffered, with millions of
his contemporaries, indelible humiliations of the Great Depression, which, following on the carnage of the Great War, would
mark British character, society, and politics for the rest of the

century. The anxiety of men, women, and children living close to the bone and the abyss is a climate of the early fiction, which frequently takes place in wet, cold, sunless settings; in which even the astute can expect little advancement and no quarter, and the rich exist in privileged unconcern. Greene's own bleak experiences in Depression years are noted in his two volumes of autobiography, and his biographer Norman Sherry records the keen relief of Graham and his young wife over a gift of ten shillings from an aunt who was herself in pinched circumstances. Vivien Greene told Sherry that, in those years at the brink, "we were very frightfully poor . . . much poorer than anyone of our own social quality." With his knowledge of that wretchedness and reduction, Graham, like others, long sought to keep faith.

Reflected in the early writings, an innermost sense of helplessness under fate and unfairness contributed to an imprudent belief, among readers, in Graham's unconditional solidarity with the underdog and the working class. Graham's sympathies—innately mercurial and unbiddable, and ever more dispassionate with age—lay far less with categories than with the peculiarities and torments of all manner of unquiet spirits in their disillusion, equivocation, culpability, self-doubt, and self-disgust. Singularity engaged him. He was disinclined to solidarity or to any sustained "position." In his books, there is culmination in the narrative, but he does not seek to "resolve."

In public matters, the maverick was, intentionally and necessarily, more exposed. Julian Symons, a literary critic who wrote, over years, appreciatively and perceptively of Greene and his work, gave his opinion, in reviewing in 1989 a volume of Graham's letters to the press, that these are the letters of a man concerned with the minor inequities and major iniquities of Western society, and ready to use his prestige as a writer to ask awkward questions and publicize uncomfortable facts. A congenital distrust of merits has prevented Graham Greene from adopting the explicitly political stance of a Günter Grass, but nobody reading these letters could doubt where his social sympathies lie.

I think that is manifestly if inconsistently true—even if the attribution of "social sympathies" might have prompted Graham to throw a spanner in the works. Again, it was rather that he "felt the loyalty we all feel to unhappiness—the sense that that is where we really belong."

Graham had known well, or intimately, or casually, a great diversity of women and men, among them oddities celebrated or obscure. In general, he required stimulus from his companions, but his familiars included an occasional adulator or sycophant; and these, though few, did not displease him. Women should show, ideally, a domestic calm and a compliant attention, or risk being found shrewish. In regard to his work, he could be canny about deploying connections; but there were compartments to his life, and some of his preoccupations had no reason to intersect. His political interventions were of a lone and intractable character; while the crowded milieu of the theatre, of which he had close experience, never lost its appeal for him. A suggestion made since his death, that he sought to know rich and powerful people, is fantastical: he did not seek people out, least of all for cachet. Prominent persons were eager to know him, not the other way round. According to mood, he was curious to meet some fresh personality, from any quarter, who might enliven an hour or an evening; and in such chance acquaintances he took an unaffected interest—that could, however, easily wane.

Graham cared nothing for fashionable life. In the drear stringency of war's-end England, the ease and charm of Catherine Walston's married setting no doubt contributed to the initial glamour of that love affair and to the confident power of a Circe from Rye, New York: a beautiful girl who had married Henry Walston, a wealthy Englishman of homely appearance and progressive politics, borne five children, and, still young, secured Graham as her trophy lover, holding him in thrall between rapture and the rack for fifteen years. Catherine was vibrant, generous, original. In her ambience, Graham met personalities of the day, not merely prominent but interesting; and aspects of his daily existence were simplified. The contrast between his own austere requirements and her social spirit is nevertheless made plain in the fine novel *The End of the Affair*, where the writer works in a lone room "across the Common" from the comfortable, busy house of his beloved and her polite, political husband.

In these matters, Graham's life and work speak for themselves. As to the insinuation that he cultivated people for their position or possessions, anyone who knew him will find it laughable.

Graham Greene's first literary successes were short-circuited by misfortunes, some of them self-inflicted. And when, with a wife and two children to support, he did reach a degree of financial security—supplementing his fiction with a crushing burden of salaried journalistic tasks—the Second World War convulsed the globe; calling populations to arms, and sweeping Greene, in his mid-thirties, into its maw. As Graham observed, he was over forty before he could afford to write on his own terms. By then, he had established himself through the development and gruelling application of his talent and intellect. He had served his apprenticeship.

Money brought freedom. By nature ascetic and in some respects parsimonious, Graham had little taste for luxury and none whatever for pretension. We merely saw that he lived where, and as sparely, as he chose; stayed, without apology, in a good hotel when it suited him; bestowed money as he saw fit and without display. By the time we met, he had already made his headquarters at Antibes, in a small modern flat near his companion of later years, Yvonne Cloetta, who, with her husband and daughters, lived close by. In addition to the Anacapri house, he had a Paris flat—which, finding that we were then much in France, he offered for our use during his absences. (Within few years, Graham had lent that Paris flat, for her lifetime, to his French literary agent, Marie Biche Schebeko, who was in rather frail health. She lived there, with her husband, until her death.) From time to time, in divesting mood, Graham would speak of selling the Rosaio—perhaps to remind himself that he could, if he chose, do so. Possessions, long regarded with suspicion, had by now been repudiated as an encumbrance. The only "purchases" ever mentioned to us were books acquired during visits to Britain when, driven by his younger brother Hugh, Graham would make descents on secondhand bookshops in the Wye Valley.

(In 1975, as Graham's "rediscovered" biography of Lord Rochester—a manuscript from 1931—was published, a double portrait by Sir Peter Lely came up for auction in New York, advertised, with photograph, as "The Countess of Rochester and another lady [said to be Nell Gwynn]." We mailed the notice to Graham at Antibes, and he replied: "Sotheby's attribution does seem a very odd one. I wish I had the money to buy the picture! I wonder what it fetched." The portrait sold for $4,000.)

Malcolm Muggeridge wrote of Graham: "Whatever his circumstances, he has this facility for seeming always to be in lodgings, and living from hand to mouth. Spiritually, and even physically, he is one of nature's displaced persons." He was not attached, through habit or memory, or aesthetically, to the rooms and houses and neighbourhoods of his life, and could throw them over at will. Familiarity bred restlessness or rejection. Even in a chosen setting, such as the Rosaio, he retained the quality of wanderer.

Indignation that would not be roused by a degree of industrial wealth no novelist could ever envisage will regularly be directed at the prosperity—rare enough—of a gifted writer. And Graham Greene, since his death, has been rebuked by commentators eager to demonstrate that, in his having caused millions of readers to buy his books throughout half a century, and having profited from that seemingly harmless transaction, he had relinquished his immortal soul. Creative writing, which, alone among the arts, seems delusively accessible to every articulate person, has immemorially attracted that confusion of esteem and envy, centred on the independence in which it is conceived and composed: a mystery of originality that never loses fascination for the onlooker. In W. H. Auden's view,

> this fascination is not due to the nature of art itself, but to the way in which an artist works; he, and in our age almost nobody else, is his own master. The idea of being one's own master appeals to most human beings, and this is apt to lead to the fantastic hope that the capacity for artistic creation is universal, something nearly all human beings, by virtue not of some special talent, but of their humanity, could do if they tried.

I think that independence and absolute freedom in the conduct of his life were imperative to Graham Greene; and that any restriction, unless self-imposed, was not only galling to him, as to many high-strung natures, but intolerable. The most difficult elements of his personality usually turned on that issue. Resentment of a real or fancied imposition, or the inability to prevail in his view or desire, could ignite a sense of infringement that seemed like madness. In certain enkindled moods, the inconsequential supposition of a shared opinion might be angrily repelled as importunate; while the failure—particularly by a woman—to fall in with his judgment could be a betrayal. In discussion, most people depend on at least a few common assumptions, if only to ensure that conversation does not founder in mindless wrangling. But reliance of that kind was just what Graham could not stand. *Agape* was his idea of hell.

All that was yet to be observed and experienced.

❧

On that afternoon in Anacapri so many years ago, we talked about the Vietnam War—then in full spate, as it would be for years thereafter. All of us deplored the war as excruciating folly, and Graham questioned Francis and me about measures taken by people like ourselves, living in the United States, to contest it. Mass protests against the war by persons of all ages and professions were, at that time, only beginning in America. In following years, as the conflict was bitterly protracted, Vietnam became an inevitable theme of our talk and our correspondence.

As we were leaving the Rosaio, in declining light, for the serpentine bus ride down the mountain, Graham pointed out the small white studio in which he worked. It was lying, like a beached boat or some marine habitation of the Peggottys, at the upper end of his walled garden. On a subsequent visit, he showed us its tiny cabin-like interior. There was still, then, the wooden floor originally installed for silence and winter warmth. I recall narrow bookshelves within arched niches, where poets were aligned in short elderly volumes together with sets of pocket-sized anthologies and Temple Shakespeares—all orderly, well cared for. There was a small divan, a chair, a lightweight portable typewriter on a solid old table by a window that looked on the garden. And there was the inexorable breath of Capri damp. It was a fine place to write: indrawn, inviolable—a refuge within the retreat, and all within an island.

Graham was to leave Capri just before the New Year. In intervening days, we dined together at Gemma several times before going our diverse ways. One evening in the restaurant, soon after we were seated, a gently mannered Swedish visitor—possibly associated with the Axel Munthe enterprise at Villa San Michele, which draws countless Scandinavian, German, and other tourists to Anacapri each year—came from a nearby table and, begging our pardon for the interruption, asked to shake Graham's hand; a fine-boned, tweedy, herring-like figure with a Sandburg cowlick of white hair, who, as Graham attempted to rise, told him, "Mr. Greene, I want to thank you for the pleasure of your books."

GG: I'm glad you like them.

SWEDISH GENT: I also wish to apologise for the fact that once again, this year, my country has failed to award you its prize.

GG: Not at all.

SG, earnestly: Perhaps next year.

GG, oracular: No. Next year, Patrick White.

SG, perplexed: Is that certain?

GG: Absolutely.

(The following year, Aleksandr Solzhenitsyn was awarded the Nobel Prize in Literature—Patrick White being, as gossip had it, the runner-up. White received the prize in 1973, donating the money to create a continuing award for Australian writers. White and Greene, who were not acquainted, maintained a mildly competitive interest in each other's careers. When we returned from a trip to Australia in 1976, Graham—learning that we were friendly with Patrick White and had visited him at Sydney—questioned us about Patrick's manner of living, and was curious as to whether the principles of material simplicity advanced in the books were reflected in the life. They were.)

There was another evening when Graham brought with him a Capri personality, Dr. Elisabeth Moor—the Viennese "Dottoressa Moor," who would become the "Impossible Woman" of Graham's later memoir and an acknowledged source for his novel *Travels with My Aunt.* A squat, categorical figure, formless in winter bundling, the Dottoressa had the rugged, russet complexion of northerners long weathered in the hot south, prominent paleolithic teeth, and memorably pale blue eyes. She was wearing a grey mock-Astrakhan fez, and did not take it off. As we sat down together, Graham told her, "You look just like Khrushchev"—which, though accurate, pleased her. Khrushchev was something of a ploy with Graham at the time. On the previous evening, we had been speaking of prescient themes in novels. I had said that the illusory "atomic" constructions concocted by the vacuum-cleaner salesman in *Our Man in Havana* prefigured the Cuban Missile Crisis of 1962. And Graham had responded: "Yes. Khrushchev got that from me." One had always assumed so.

The Dottoressa Moor had evidently not expected to share Graham with unknown others, and made displeasure plain—barely acknowledging Francis and ignoring me altogether. Over dinner, Graham seemed amused by her surly directives. Possessive of his attention and flattered by it, she showed him a truculent devotion. They had known each other from Graham's first visits to Capri, meeting through Norman Douglas, one of whose last doctors she had been; and Graham had given her solidarity during a series of cruel private tragedies. With her belligerence and self-praise, and her gratuitous rudeness, she could not immediately endear herself to Francis or to me. Only the eyes were incongruous—anxious, appealing, the very colour of girlishness.

Graham was inclined to assign parts to subsidiary players in his drama (and to take it amiss when they forgot their lines or deviated from their role). The Dottoressa had clearly enlisted as a character, the Impossible Woman of the subsequent script: "You are right, I am a wild one." As far as we were concerned, she did not strike one as quite impossible enough: more like an amateur at impossibility. Whereas Graham was a pro: a formidable master of the impossible.

Years afterwards, writing to Michael Richey, I mentioned in a postscript the Dottoressa's unprovoked hostility on that evening. Richey replied: "I was amused by your note about the Dottoressa. I don't think she liked women. She loved Graham of course and he was immensely kind to her." Michael told me that once, in Rome, Graham had spent seven hours at the airport in order to see the aged Dottoressa safely aboard her belated plane: "Most people would have left her."

In regard to her projected memoirs, the Dottoressa had written: "I would like to live in a state of men only. Women should be eradicated." She did her best in that direction throughout our dinner together. Ultimately, the evening we spent with her at Gemma was to have a sequel.

❧

On an afternoon following Christmas, Francis ran into Graham in one of the little Capri streets, and together they came to join me where I was reading indoors in the Gran Caffè. As they sat down at the table, I closed my book; and Graham, saying, "May I see what you're reading?," took it from my hand. The moment is vivid— early dark, and the lamps yellowish; wintry silence in the square; the two long-limbed men seated on small cane chairs; the three of us drawn together. And Graham's tone, gentler than I was almost ever to hear it—one would say, seductively so. And his extended, extraordinary hand turning the book.

It was a work congenial to the Edwardian and Georgian aspects of his taste: Edmund Gosse's *Father and Son*. (I later saw, in one of Graham's collections of travel essays, that it was among books he had taken to West Africa during the war.) He said, "Yes, it's very good, isn't it? You even come to like the father. There's some loss of control near the end, but it hardly matters." Of his own father, Graham, like Gosse, had developed more lenient memories— occasionally expressed in dreams, as he relates in *A Sort of Life*.

Graham's loyalty to those turn-of-the-century writers, the literary elders of his boyhood, was, though discriminating, nearly familial. He was not in the least intimidated by the opprobrium heaped—for generations now, and collectively—on the Georgian poets; and was pleased when once I quoted lines, which he recognized, written in the South Seas in 1913 by the arch-offender, Rupert Brooke:

> *As who would pray good for the world, but know*
> *Their benediction empty as they bless.*

Greene has recounted the excitement of the "adventure" writers he had read in early youth—Henty, Haggard, Hornung, Kipling, Stevenson, Conan Doyle. His own writings testify to that influence, as did his life. One book, uncompromising and unclassifiable, had cast an enduring spell:

> When—perhaps I was fourteen by that time—I took Miss Marjorie Bowen's *The Viper of Milan* from the library shelf, the future for better or for worse really struck. From that moment I began to write . . . One could not read her without believing that to write was to live and to enjoy.

The Viper of Milan was published in 1906, when its author was a girl of sixteen. It remained a staple of British bookcases for generations, and was on our own shelves in my childhood. I have it still: a historical novel of the wars between the dukes of Verona and Milan ("Millun," as we then pronounced it), with some of the flavour and detachment of Stendhal's stories of those violent and prodigious times. A calm mingling of charm and horror sustains the reader's attention and dread: on a spring night in a moonlit garden, the fragrant wallflowers are "the colour of blood just dry." As Graham has suggested, the book made evil interesting.

Graham read, also, the popular periodicals of stories for boys, staples of the time. In my childhood, we had huge old bound volumes of *Chums* that came from my father: issues from 1914 to 1917, their chivalrous and whimsical tone, and their jingoism, steadily challenged by realities of the Great War. (My father, like thousands of others, presumably went straight from reading those high-hearted tales of resourcefulness and honour to the trenches, where he arrived at the age of seventeen.) In the stories, there was much hiding and disguising, much suspense of being sought and caught, or of narrowly eluding discovery, a contest of quick-wittedness that would have particularly pleased the boy Greene. Plots were sel-dom original: with fair frequency, there was the irrepressible, all-betraying sneeze in the dusty attic, or the pepper flung in the assailant's eyes. Through pluck and ingenuity, the slim young hero prevailed in the end, and made light of his triumph.

Heading once for an appointment with a troublesome relative, Graham told us: "I'm taking a screw of pepper in my pocket, just in case he gets violent."

In *The Quiet American*, arcane and drastic allusion is made, I think, to those stories of his boyhood, when the narrator, hiding in a rice paddy, feels a sneeze fatally coming on:

> But in the very second that my sneeze broke, the Viets opened with Stens, drawing a line of fire through the rice . . .

A thoroughly Greene-ish juxtaposition of encoded sentiment and lethal violence; quite worthy of Miss Marjorie Bowen.

Graham has described how his first reading of stories, as child and schoolboy, took place in solitary retreats of home and gar-den—corners of the comfortable, confident England that shel-tered complicated and talented families like the Greenes in the early part of the twentieth century. Aspects of that world in which his infancy and troubled schooldays were passed—a world whose judgments were invoked with scorn and pain in his youth-ful fiction—had remained, or become, pleasing to him; and its emblems were densely if scabrously assembled, in 1975, for his last play, *The Return of A. J. Raffles*, which he styled "An Edwardian Comedy." The period and its literary adventurers—wayfarers, explorers, sleuths, remittance men, double agents—had their permanent place in his consciousness: enigmatic, clandestine, or seedy originals who outclassed, for Graham, those forthright soldier and sailor heroes, representatives of empire and team spirit, who provided national exemplars in an era extinguished by the First World War.

Graham's volatile attachments were, as he intended, always hard to call—even in regard to causes to which he generally adhered. However, on the theme of his upbringing, he might on a good day have endorsed Auden's acknowledgment that

> *The class whose vices he pilloried was his own,*
> *now extinct, except*
> *for lone survivors like him*
> *who remember its virtues.*

We parted in late December with the expectation of meeting again on Capri in the spring. Graham told us, "I'm glad I forgot that line of Browning."

After Graham's departure, Michael, Francis, and I dined together a last time at Gemma on New Year's Eve. It was a cold clear night such as Rilke spent on Capri on the eve of the year 1907—climbing to the roof of his little house in the garden of Villa Discopoli to see "an earth of moonlight, of moon shadow":

And the night was a bright, distant one that seemed to rest above far more than just the earth; one felt that it lay above oceans and far out beyond, above space, above itself, above stars . . .

In the same oceanic silence, Francis and I walked at evening along the deserted Tragara path, high above the sea, past the "Moorish" Villa Discopoli, which had not then been transformed into a costly condominium. Returning to the piazza and reaching the restaurant, we were startled by unprecedented holiday numbers and by hilarity that, as midnight neared, was swelled by the traditional itinerant group of costumed Capresi singers making hay with tambourines and with their curious traditional instruments derived from a remote past—"a weird, barbaric affair," as D. H. Lawrence saw it, on the eve of the new year 1920, when he, in his literary turn, was wintering on Capri.

Those outlandish instruments, some of them suggestively indecent in appearance and operation, have old dialect names: the *putipù,* the *triccaballacco,* and the *scètavajasse* (or "slut-waker"). The *putipù,* in size and aspect like a smallish portable drum with one central perforation, seems to have found its way round the Mediterranean since pagan times. In *South from Granada,* Gerald Brenan describes its miniature, and primitive, Spanish counterpart:

The last festival of the year was Christmas . . . It was the solstice. The only special feature was the appearance of that disagreeable noise-making instrument, the *zambomba.* This consists of a piece of rabbit-skin or goat-skin drawn tight across the mouth of a broken flower-pot or drainpipe: a stick is inserted through the skin and, after the hand has been wetted, is pushed up and down, so that it gives a half-squeaking, half-moaning sound. The sexual significance is obvious, and no doubt it was originally intended as a magical rite to give strength to the declining sun. In Yegen it was chiefly the young men who performed upon it, and, when girls were present, they did so with a conscious gusto, and among much tittering and laughter. In the towns it has now sunk to being a children's toy.

There has been no such falling-off in Capri. The *putipù* holds its own on festive and touristic occasions, wielded "with conscious gusto" not only by young men but also by pretty laughing girls with long coloured ribbons in their hair.

We came back to Capri in the following spring. So did Graham. He appeared one May evening at Gemma's fireside while we were dining with two friends at our usual table. With him was Yvonne Cloetta, who had on a leash her golden spaniel, Sandy. It was Yvonne's presence at Antibes that had caused Graham to move there from England in the 1960s, following their first meeting, in Africa, in 1959.

No pretty woman was ever more suited than Yvonne to the adjective *petite*. Heart-shaped smiling face, short shock of strong white hair; slight, perfectly proportioned compact body dressed in trousers and a pastel shirt, with a shawl at evening. Good English, spoken with charming accent, made her an invaluable amanuensis to Graham at Antibes. A use of Italian enabled her to act, also, as intermediary during their Capri visits.

Yvonne loved—one might say, idolised—Graham. On her love that moody man had established a reliance that endured through the last thirty years of his life. Seeing them together, hearing his tone to her, one found it impossible to imagine, in their attachment, the anguish or antagonism that had otherwise characterised, since youth, Graham's relations with women.

On that spring evening of their return, there was the welcome from the staff of the restaurant, where Graham had dined since the late 1940s; where he was addressed by the personnel, incongruously, as Signor Grin—and by Gemma herself, who spoke no English, as Grahmgrin, or Grahm. The unaltered simplicity of Gemma's restaurant was a stable factor that helped make the island agreeable to Graham. Like many restless people, he preferred to find his ports of call unchanged. For Gemma, who would stand for a moment by his table, holding both his hands and smiling, Graham had an unusual degree of trust and fondness; and I think that this was not solely due to the fact that they could exchange no words. Gemma's benign composure drew many of her clients to the restaurant throughout their lifetime and hers.

She had founded the restaurant in the 1930s, with her husband, who was for many years the chef. Born into the rustic life of bodily labour usual to Capresi of her generation, she was one of a large family whose centre and support she became while still young. Two, and then three, generations of relatives were deployed in the restaurant, and Gemma's fisherman brother masterminded the day's catch. Gemma sometimes spoke of her parents, of their resilience under a hard life and the exigencies of numerous children. She spoke to us, too, of the famished years of the Second World War, when the island's produce was impounded for the armed forces and when, with the wholesale bombardments of Naples in 1943 and 1944—monstrously compounded by the eruption of Vesuvius in March 1944—crowds of poor Neapolitans rowed themselves out to Capri, vainly seeking sustenance and shelter.

Gemma's calm diffused itself through her restaurant even in the high season, from mid-June to late September, when the large, glassed summer room, with grand view, was afloat with the colours worn by couples and families on holiday, and with the shimmer of fashionable figures who arrived to dine near midnight.

If Graham delayed his spring or autumn visit, Gemma would ask if we had news of his return. When Francis, who had much affection for Gemma, once teased her, "Graham is more precious to you than I am," she replied: "It's true. He needs it more."

At Gemma's death, in 1984, Graham walked in her funeral procession.

On one of his earliest visits to Capri, Graham and Catherine had come unexpectedly to the island over Christmas, only to find everything closed on Christmas Day, including Gemma. At the Rosaio, Carmelina was spending the holy day with her family. "Discovering that we had nowhere to dine or buy food, Gemma asked us to Christmas dinner at her house. We were placed at her table, and found that no one else would sit down. The entire family waited on us, and nothing would induce them to join us."

Francis said, "You were the honoured guests. Something nearly Oriental."

"Yes. We sat enthroned like the pampered jades of Asia, and were served with all those dishes."

When "Catherine" came up, it was often in some recollection of Italy: "We were at Sirmione one summer, on our way back to

England, and Catherine realised that she needed a hat for a Palace garden party the next day. At Sirmione she bought a straw hat off a stall. It cost eight shillings. She got the hat, and she wore it to Buck House."

ॐ

We began, from that time, a pattern loosely followed for many years—of meeting in spring and autumn when we were usually, all four, on Capri—Graham and Yvonne coming for a month or so, Francis and I for longer. Occasionally, we went up to the Rosaio for lunch, finding the house open to fine weather, and the garden—like all the island's gardens in May—a riot of flowers and colours: whole hedges of white marguerites, swags of petunias and trailing geraniums, electric-blue lobelia, trellised roses, and groups of amaryllis, pale or crimson—a radiance within white walls that was the work of Aniello, Carmelina's husband. In autumn, when we often lunched at the Rosaio for Graham's birthday on the second of October, there were tawny colours of the island's late reflowering. Sometimes we arrived at evening, for a drink, before dining outdoors at an Anacapri trattoria, La Rondinella, where Graham reserved the one secluded table. In our early years of friendship, Graham and Yvonne once in a while came down from the Monte Solaro and made the stiff climb, of paths and steps, to lunch on our own covered terrace. More rarely, Graham might propose lunch by the sea, or a walk ending at a small restaurant. But our habitual place was Gemma, at evening. It was an easy arrangement: we turned up independently, usually without fixed appointment—Francis and I sometimes staying away so that

Graham and Yvonne might dine by themselves. It was very pleasant, putting work aside at the end of the day, changing into fresh clothes, strolling to the piazza in that scene of sky and sea: the late light, the expectation of interest and pleasure, the welcome at the restaurant, where we all preferred to dine, by south Italian summer standards, quite early.

By the time we knew him on Capri, Graham was not a heavy drinker. He and Yvonne might share a bottle of the Sicilian wine Corvo—"I like the name"—or of rosé from Ravello. We were light eaters of traditional dishes, of fish or shellfish from those waters. None of us gave first importance to food, or tended to discuss it at length—though Graham might occasionally hark back to a bad or costly meal eaten elsewhere, some episode rankling from the long past ("I still remember the severe price of a picnic lunch provided by the hotel" being his recorded impression of a postwar trip to Athens). Asceticism played its part in his paradox.

While the evening excursion to Gemma's restaurant was pleasurable to Graham, I think that for him the imperative of food remained something of a tyranny. He was preternaturally resistant to any form of compulsion; and nothing is more peremptory than the digestive system. Early in life, according to his memoirs, he had rebelled against the fixed hours of meals ("There is a charm in improvised eating which a regular meal lacks"). In childhood, he would steal currants and raisins from the school supply and "stuff my pockets with them, currants in the left, sultanas in the right, and feast on them secretly in the garden"—with queasy consequences, for "the meal ended always with a sensation of nausea, but to be secure from detection I had to finish them all, even the strays which had picked up fluff from the seams of the pockets."

In the fiction, food is almost always an unfavourable portent, invoked vengefully and with revulsion, or in regard to an unmasking. In *The Heart of the Matter,* there is the unwanted and distasteful lunch—"an enormous curry which filled a washing-basin in the middle of the table"—served to Scobie and his hapless wife as she takes ship for Durban. In *The End of the Affair,* there is "the hideous meal" that Bendrix obliges the cuckolded Henry Miles to share with him (Henry having been dished, early in the story, over a plate of onions). At the ghastly lunch, Henry "was too ill at ease to comment on the dish and somehow he managed to ram the pink soggy mixture down." *Our Man in Havana,* for his part, survives a murderous banquet of Chicken Maryland by giving his poisoned drink to the beloved dachshund of a sinister waiter. ("The dog collapsed at the waiter's feet and lay there like a length of offal.") The dog of Pyle, the Quiet American, has a tongue "like a burnt pancake." The cowed dinner guests of the sadistic Dr. Fischer of Geneva force themselves to down the cold porridge that causes one of them to vomit. At Dr. Fischer's, we have already learned, "the dinners are abominable."

Aversions to food have prompted knowing comment since antiquity, and interpretations are not lacking in our own assiduous day. However that may be, Graham's "case" was consistent with his hostility to all matters imposed on him—whether by circumstance or natural forces, or at the will of others: a motif unmistakable in the pattern of years. The helplessness or complicity of our humanity in its involuntary needs, cravings, and decay aroused a resentment conspicuous above all in many of Graham's responses to women. For much of his life he had wrestled, in love and in his books, with the paradox of desire and consummation, illusion and disgust, ecstasy and blame. It was not difficult to imagine him holding the view ascribed by Plutarch to Alexander the Great—another abstemious eater—that "sleep and the act of generation chiefly made him sensible that he was merely mortal."

❧

Repeatedly singled out as a writer of his "era," Graham, even so, long eluded literary chronology. His best work, with its disarming blend of wit, event, and lone fatality, has not staled; and he himself, always ready, with eager scepticism, for life's next episode, did not seem to "date." However, in one respect—his attitudes to women—he remained rooted, as man and writer, in his early decades.

From the 1920s into the 1940s, Greene and several of his talented male contemporaries were working, in English fiction, related veins of anxiety and intelligence, anger and danger, sex and sensibility, and contrasting an ironic private humanity with the petty vanities and great harm of established power. Their narrative frequently centred on the difficulty of being a moody, clever, thin-skinned—and occasionally alcoholic—literate man who commands the devotion of a comely, plucky, self-denying younger woman. These were demonstrable elements of educated life in Britain between the sexes and between the wars, and they lingered in Graham's fiction ever after, briefly "orientalised" in *The Quiet American*.

In the characterisation of women, the male novelists of those years wrote as though Elizabeth Bennet, Dorothea Brooke, Becky Sharp, and Emma Bovary had never been created. Woman, ideally, should be the handmaid of man, or sexually disposable. In his collection of essays, *Enemies of Promise*, Cyril Connolly addresses the grim fate of good writers—for him, exclusively male—who are misguided enough to marry, a pitfall alleviated only by sufficient fortune and a wife with no hankerings for self-fulfilment:

> a wife who is intelligent and unselfish enough to understand and respect the working of the unfriendly cycle of the creative imagination. She will know at what point domestic happiness begins to cloy, where love, tidiness, rent, rates, clothes, entertainings and rings at the doorbell should stop and will recognise that there is no more sombre enemy of good art than the pram in the hall.

This passage so exactly expressed Graham Greene's own sentiments that he invoked it, in *The Quiet American*, through his ageing protagonist, the journalist Fowler, who is out East in flight from British suburbia—from "the kind of house that has no mercy—a broken tricycle stood in the hall." Fowler's diminutive young Vietnamese mistress, Phuong, is a toy for her lover, present in his room or his bed when he needs her, and otherwise obligingly non-existent. As Phuong prepares Fowler's opium pipe, "she lay at my feet like a dog on a crusader's tomb."

Both Connolly and Greene had long and extravagantly unhappy affairs—and, in Connolly's case, a marriage—with handsome, dynamic women utterly removed, in temperament and ambition, from that fictional domestic ideal. The congested English hallway of prams and tricycles drove Graham and his characters to far-off places; but the dream of womanly self-effacement never ceased to haunt his work. In *The End of the Affair*, Sarah Miles is drawn from Catherine Walston, who, in her husband's house, lived in

wealth and ease among the influential figures of her time. The fictitious Sarah, whose married circumstances are similarly privileged,
contemplates the happier existence she might enjoy if she left her
long-suffering husband for her short-tempered lover, who is a
writer. Sarah, still young, has no thought of developing, in changed
conditions, her own latent qualities. Instead, she reflects: "On typ-
ing alone, with me to help, we should save fifty pounds a year."

Rose, in *Brighton Rock*, is literally ready to die for love: "I'll do
anything for you. Tell me what to do." Rose, in the play *The Living
Room*, does die for love, taking her own life: "Just say what you
want. I'm awfully obedient." In Graham's early fiction, ability is suspect. Girls can be humorous and lively, but never proficient. When
Louise, the tiresome, tearful wife of Scobie in *The Heart of the
Matter*, proposes to get a wartime job, her husband, a good man,
responds, "I hope we shall be able to manage without that." Scobie's
mistress, Helen, is, at nineteen, reassuringly incompetent: "I'm not
really any good at anything." Rescued from a lifeboat, Helen has
been installed in a prefabricated hut, where Scobie visits her. Loving
him, she is figuratively shipwrecked, without purposes or prospects. Helplessness is her attraction: "He never forgot how she was
carried into his life on a stretcher." This time, it is the hero, Scobie,
who, torn between two dependent women, takes his own life.

Henry, which was the given name of Catherine Walston's husband, was heartlessly bestowed by Graham on the betrayed and
ludicrous husband in *The End of the Affair,* the novel, intense as
a love letter, which, originating in Graham's first years with

Catherine, was published in 1951—when that affair, far from ending, had still a decade to run. Henry Walston, whose gentle complaisance throughout Catherine's various infidelities and, in particular, during the extended drama with Graham invites incredulity, maintained a long "policy" of tolerance, kindness, and submission, apparently founded on the belief that his beautiful wife would never leave him. In that conviction he was ultimately vindicated; though one can hardly call it winning. Meantime, the afflicted Henry Scobie of *The Heart of the Matter* had given place to a series of pusillanimous Henrys—Henry Miles, Henry Pulling, "poor Henry" Hawthorne ("I wish you wouldn't call him Henry")— all marked down for ridicule in Graham's fiction, where Henry had become a byword for naïveté and impotence.

Henry was also Graham's own name. In the autumn of 1904, the year of his birth, Graham had been christened Henry Graham Greene. He had known some early use of that first name, into his twenties. With Graham, no such play of circumstance could be inadvertent.

During one of our early reunions on Capri, Graham asked Francis whether there were "more letters from Egypt." We were sitting outdoors in the Gran Caffè, *à quatre,* before dinner, and Graham was speaking of Francis's translations of letters of Gustave Flaubert that had appeared in 1954—a selection that was the forerunner of extensive annotated volumes of Flaubert's correspondence published by F. in later years. Francis assured Graham that there was indeed more Oriental material—letters, journals, other commentary: "a lot of good stuff," some of it previously considered unpublishable in English because of its indecency, an inhibition since dissolved by transformations of mores and, in Britain, by the *Lady Chatterley* trial of 1959.

Graham said that, among publishers, indecency was now becoming "a competition rather than an obstacle." (I remember that he added, with reference to his own work, "I don't do much of that, myself.") He proposed that, if Francis would undertake to translate and edit an expanded account of Flaubert's Eastern travels of 1849–50, he would arrange to publish it with The Bodley Head, the London firm of which he was a director. The book became *Flaubert in Egypt,* first appearing in 1972. Francis liked to look back on its genesis, settled in few words over a whisky on a May night in the little piazza of Capri. Flaubert himself, at Naples in 1851 during the return journey from his Near Eastern trip, had been, as he put it, "set on going to Capri; and very nearly remained there—in the deep," having narrowly survived a squall on a stormy sea. As the site of Graham's literary suggestion, the island might be seen as offering a late gesture of atonement in Flaubert's direction.

By then, Graham had a consultant's role at The Bodley Head, not concerning himself with the daily business of the firm but continuing to bring writers to its list. He read manuscripts and— from habit and for pleasure—a wide sweep of new books and reviews. The book pages of *The Observer* and *The Sunday Times*— whose regular reviewers were then Graham's literary contemporaries—were sought with unjaded curiosity each Monday from the Anacapri newsstand, and would be mentioned at dinner. Among American publications, Graham habitually saw *The New Yorker* and *The New York Review of Books*—*The New Yorker*, where his work had only once appeared, coming in for some blunt reproof. (That brief story, "Men at Work," published in 1941, satirically depicts, against the backdrop of blitzed and embattled London, the sententious irrelevance of a ministerial meeting: a theme that, freely and ironically aired in wartime British writings, achieved its apotheosis in 1943, with Nigel Balchin's masterly little novel, *The Small Back Room*.)

A review by A. J. Liebling of *The Quiet American*, published in *The New Yorker* of April 7, 1956, legitimately rankled, and came up in our earliest conversation about the Vietnam War. Naïve and punitive, the review dismissed the possibility that a United States government would engage in death-dealing intrigue, and condemned the author's irresponsibility as conscious evil. Even in the earnest America of that era, it was a memorably obtuse piece of writing from an experienced journalist; and Graham spoke of it with his particular smile conveying contempt and rage. The magazine's subsequent and eloquent exposures of America's recklessness in Southeast Asia gratified him, but could not atone.

I had kept Liebling's article from the time of its publication, as if expecting it to account for itself. It never did. Twenty years, and a long war, later, I gave it to a friend who was writing on Vietnam.

Graham's years in journalism and publishing had sharpened an eye and ear not only for fresh talent but for what might sell. If a new book had vitality, an element of opportunism, even of trashiness, did not necessarily bother him; although his judgment was ultimately literary and his regard for language remained uncompromised. From women who wrote, he in general required some tinge of the inexorable as a countering of sensibility—some strain of the sardonic or bizarre, or of a nearly asexual astringency, such as he had first singled out in *The Viper of Milan.* He could weigh in heavily against irreverent female depictions of relations between the sexes, and rather mistrusted expositions of love written by intelligent women. When he told me that he had never read *Pride and Prejudice,* it was with the implication that he didn't intend to.

Promptly generous with time and public praise for new books that pleased him, he brought enthusiasm to his reading. A fresh book never ceased to be a possibility, a promise. It was, I think, his only consistent form of optimism.

Although Graham took exception to the designation of "Catholic writer" or "Catholic novelist" applied to himself in the press, he did have special curiosity about fiction in which Catholicism figured; and a number of his younger writing protégés and preferences were Catholic. He retained, too, a taste for books of "pilgrimage," about difficult adventures in the world's disregarded byways. Our responses to books mostly coincided—and almost always with respect to the past; but Graham had unappealable antipathies, his curt condemnations being of a vehemence that discouraged discussion. In the contemporary torrent of new books, he kept a clear memory of work he had liked—a single novel, an obscure memoir, a collection of trenchant stories—and bore the author's name long in mind. Finding that we knew the novelist Frank Tuohy, who had for a time fallen silent, Graham asked, with indignation, "And what about Tuohy? Where is Tuohy? Tuohy's good." His own productivity, unbroken almost to the end, made him impatient of the lapses of others.

Hard-headed about profitable publishing, Graham nevertheless felt, as a matter of course, the writer's point of view. When he learned that a young writer whom he had brought with success to The Bodley Head had soon been let go, he told us: "They said his new manuscript wasn't his best. But one can't always be at one's best."

Graham relied on Max Reinhardt, who directed The Bodley Head, to maintain the character and prosperity of the firm. He also looked to Reinhardt, more personally, for ballast and discretion. In March 1972, when the Italian publisher Giangiacomo Feltrinelli was killed—apparently by an explosive device related to Feltrinelli's own clandestine ventures—Graham wrote to us that one would prefer one's publisher to represent stability: "I don't see Max blown up under a pylon."

Graham Greene did not come to Capri as earlier generations of foreign writers and artists had done, accessible to the island's history and beauty, and curious for new experience there. If most of his travels were acknowledged ways of escape, his Capri visits in particular were a means of being "away"—from routine and interruptions, and from the consequent menace of *accidie,* at his headquarters in Antibes. And a means, too, of being alone with the beloved, a term that should encompass his work.

He had never remained on the island at length. That short stay in spring, and again in autumn, in the Anacapri house was occasionally preceded or followed by a few days in other Italian places already familiar to him from the past with Catherine Walston. He and Yvonne might spend a few days at Ravello, on a height above Amalfi; or in Rome, where, choosing to travel by train, they stayed overnight at the Grand Hotel near the station. Even in those brief travels, Graham did not seek serenity, and his letters often recount, without displeasure, mild disruptions of routine. ("When we arrived in Rome we found police on every floor of the Grand Hotel because the Queen was coming. In pyjamas from the bedroom window during our siesta we watched her arrival.") In the 1970s, he visited Harold Acton at Florence, and Kenneth Macpherson—an early Capri connection, through Norman Douglas—in another handsome villa, at Cetona. For Graham, Capri was a hiatus. At the Rosaio, he settled to his pages each morning—"I must do my three hundred and fifty words"—and took up the habits of his island life. It was a simulation, or as much as he could tolerate, of "home."

Graham's feelings toward the Rosaio, as to the world in general, were much subject to circumstance and state of mind. He told us that he had intermittently considered giving up the house almost since acquiring it. In the early 1970s, when he again spoke of selling the Rosaio, he conceded: "My connection with Capri is odd. It isn't really my kind of place." When Francis asked, "What is your kind of place?" there was a laugh, the shrug. "Well, not Antibes. But—*she's* there." She, by now and until the end, was Yvonne.

In Graham's first years of visiting Capri, he had had the company, when he chose, of a handful of lively and literary resident compatriots and other English-speaking visitors. He had enjoyed the last effulgence of Norman Douglas—then in his late, benevolent "Uncle Norman" phase, but entering the disabling illnesses that would cause him, in 1952, at the age of eighty-three, to take his own life. Douglas's many lives are wonderfully recounted in a biography by Mark Holloway published in Britain in 1976.

In his last years, Douglas still attracted a continuity of visitors from Britain and elsewhere—admirers of his works and, in some instances, writers themselves; and others merely curious to spend an hour with an unclassifiable and notorious figure of those still literary times. By then, Douglas was the doyen and survivor of the generations of expatriate talents from Britain and northern Europe, from Russia and America, who had sporadically lived on Capri in the nineteenth century and into the twentieth. Francis, staying on the island in 1950, several times saw the craggy old sage seated at his habitual table outside the Bar Vittoria (now the Caffè Funicolare) overlooking the bay, where he stationed himself to enjoy the Homeric scene that sweeps from Ischia on the one hand to Vesuvius on the other—with the great city extended between in a ripe tempera of Neapolitan light; its pastel palazzi, in the words of Charles Dickens at Naples, "dwindling down to dice."

At the Bar Vittoria, Douglas received the homage and the proffered wines and whiskies—all welcome in those lean years—of admiring travellers. The more considerate votaries left notes for him, to request appointments; others simply presented themselves at his table. Seeing this, Francis refrained—regretting, however, the lost, and last, opportunity for a brief encounter with that surviving fragment, as it seemed, of the pagan world: polymath, paedophile, classicist; satyr and scientist; husband, once, and father; and author of, among much else, *Old Calabria* and *Looking Back,* as he sat, in F.'s words, "handsome, humorous, incorrigible," concluding his long affair with Siren Land.

I must have heard in childhood the title of Douglas's best-known book, the novel *South Wind*. When, in adolescence, I first read it, I imagined the *scirocco* as a languorous breeze conducive to voluptuous scenes by Lawrence Alma-Tadema—whose "Roman" paintings are often set within the Bay of Naples. In my early twenties, living for the first time in Italy and at Naples, I learned the reality of that thick wind, deplored by Dante, which carries the sands of eroded Africa and an oceanic humidity into Italy—spreading red dust and black gloom before dissolving in rain; and accounting for, as Norman Douglas suggests, some outlandish local behaviour.

Douglas's funeral, on a cold day of February 1952, was attended by the Capri populace, whose menfolk—it would have been immodest, then, for women to appear at the head of a parade—walked behind the coffin in silent procession as it was carried by pallbearers from the piazza to the cemetery. Photographs convey the greyness and gravity of other times, and the solemnity of working men in their Sunday clothes: the pause occasioned by mortality. The non-Catholic section of the cemetery contains the neglected memorials of many foreigners who lived and died on the island during the past century and more. Among them, Douglas's grave is marked by a long slab of dark green marble on which his name and dates are incised, with the plain addition of a line from Horace: *Omnes Eodem Cogimur:* "Where we all must gather." The same quotation served as title for a memoir by Kenneth Macpherson written immediately after Douglas's death. Interleaved with photographs by Islay Lyons, handsomely printed, and bound in cloth appropriately purple, the book was given to friends, and later acquired by a few outsiders. Remaining copies, injudiciously stored in Capri when Macpherson left the island (first for Tuscany, and then for Thailand) were ravaged by mould.

In Douglas's last years, Macpherson had sheltered him in independent quarters in Villa Tuoro on Capri—where, with Islay Lyons, Macpherson then spent much of the year. Macpherson—a writer and filmmaker, much of whose fortune derived from his former wife, the writer "Bryher"—died in 1971. Following Lyons's death, in 1996, his heir, Manop Charoensuk, arranged for publication of a volume of his photographs, some of which again commemorate that postwar Capri of Douglas, and of Graham Greene.

Graham paid his own tribute to Douglas by writing the introduction to *Venus in the Kitchen,* an aphrodisiac cookbook that was Douglas's last work, published soon after his death. The brief foreword may be Graham's most vivid and truly affectionate portrait of a friend—"of a life consistently open, tolerant, unashamed"; of Douglas in his final months, enthroned at his table in the Bar Vittoria, at the rim of a Capri cliff,

> on the borders of the kingdom that he had built house by house, character by character, legend by legend . . . He will be delighted in the shades at any success we may have with his recipes and bark with laughter at our ignominious failures, and how pleased he will be at any annotations and additions, so long as they are exact, scholarly, uninflated, and do not carpingly arise from a cold temperament. For even his enormous tolerance had certain limits. He loved life too well to have patience with puritans or fanatics. He was a gentleman and he disliked a boor.

Acquiring the Rosaio in the period of Norman Douglas's decline, and at the onset of his own wide fame, Graham Greene might have seemed the initiator of a new wave of literary Britons on Capri. However, that particular party was over. Writers would still visit, and revisit, the island. Some would, like ourselves, become occasional residents there. But there was never again a literary or artistic "colony" of closely knit and disputatious foreigners as in the past, wearing away damp winters at each other's firesides: gossiping and quarrelling, reading and writing in an ancient and still enchanting place. Douglas had supplied a last point of reference in Capri's long expatriate continuity; and Graham had been the last notable figure to profit from it—received, at his arrival, into an easy ambience of liveliness and eccentricity that, drawn together by the presence of Douglas, would disperse with his death.

By the 1960s, that legacy of Graham's English-speaking friends on Capri had been mostly dissolved by deaths and departures. The entrepreneurial Edwin Cerio, a dominant presence on the island throughout his lifetime, died in 1960 at the age of eighty-four. Possessed of some genius, capable of generosity, Cerio—who made imaginative contributions to conservation and culture on Capri—leaves, alas, a lasting impression of opportunism and lack of principle. His father, Ignazio Cerio, a doctor from Abruzzo who settled on Capri in the 1860s and became an important and much loved benefactor of the island, was unable to transmit his own simple goodness to any of three sons, of whom Edwin was the most gifted and energetic, and the most worldly. Until his authority was overshadowed by the imperatives of fascism, Edwin Cerio reigned on Capri as a benevolent despot, entertaining dynastic ambitions—which, consummated in an obsessive acquisition of property, were thwarted by lack of a legitimate male heir.

Graham had known Cerio in postwar years, again through Douglas, and maintained his friendship with Cerio's daughter, Laetitia, for the rest of his life. An accomplished painter and linguist,

Laetitia herself became, with age, a doyenne of Capri personalities, a stylish and fastidious *grande dame,* at the centre of the island's occasions and institutions. Laetitia died in 1997, in her late eighties.

Ian Greenlees, a cultivated and independent mind, had left Capri for Florence, where he long directed the British Institute; but retained, and regularly visited, his picturesque old Anacapri house, Villa Fraita, acquired from the writer Francis Brett Young in the late 1940s. In appearance, manner, and pallor, a ringer for Sidney Greenstreet, Ian had a long past in Italy; and kept a specific—in some circles, inconvenient—memory of the country's tribulation under fascism.

Graham was fond of Gracie Fields, who shifted between her beach establishment at the Marina Piccola, on Capri's southern shore, and a house in Anacapri. Gracie had simplicity, good humour, shrewdness: a human distinction. She, too, had kept faith with early experience. Handsome, with white hair, fine eyes, she had little of the varnished performer—rather, a suggestion of vulnerability. She told me—as other women have sometimes done—that she had never had a genuinely requited love. She was sought out by tourists from Britain, and particularly from Lancashire, with whom she was generous of her time and broad smiles, and even of her songs; enjoying her fame, up to a point. When I was with Gracie, once, on an obscure path, we were stopped by a foursome from Manchester who, exacting insistent snapshots, detained her over-long. As we at last walked on, Gracie remarked, "Ah, loov, it's well to be reminded that our own lot can be as gormless as anyone else's."

Those long-lingering presences were accepted, in the Italian way, as components of the scene and contributors to its story—

together with other foreigners who had their share not necessarily of fame but of singularity.

Graham's acquaintances on Capri, seen sporadically, included the Scotsman John Cairncross, a connection from Graham's "intelligence" era, and former member of the Cambridge group of moles, from which he had long seceded. During his years with the United Nations Food and Agriculture Organization in Rome, Cairncross kept, near the Anacapri shore, a pleasant house that was sold soon after we rented our Capri rooms.

In the postwar 1940s, younger Italian novelists whose talents were emerging from the eclipse of fascist decades had become a fluctuating presence on Capri. Of these, Graham knew Mario Soldati, lover of women and wines; and Alberto Moravia, who, with his wife, the novelist Elsa Morante, was long familiar with the islands of the Neapolitan gulf and had passed a period of "banishment" in the region under fascism. Of those Italian writers, few would stay at length on the island or feel sustained desire to cluster there. (An exception was the novelist Raffaele La Capria, who later acquired a house on the steep approach to Monte Solaro.) In Europe, it was a time of political and intellectual ferment, and clustering would be done in cities. Among thinking people, the need for withdrawal and reflection was evaporating, giving place to immediacy, assertion, and public commitment. Concepts of space, time, territory were also changing. The impetus for free movement, pent up under dictatorship and war, would now become airborne—novelty, rather than revelation, being sought in brief forays into far places.

The city of Naples itself, a shambles from bombardment and from recent ravages of dictatorship and conquest, drew few visitors, then and for long thereafter. Those who came to know Naples in that era, however, would feel an attachment to it all their lives.

Northerners in search of southern sun and permissiveness were still drawn, as in past centuries, to the beautiful surroundings of Naples; but there was some feeling that Capri, so long renowned, must have staled. Independent travellers who strayed along those coasts now lodged themselves, rather, in crannies near Positano or Amalfi, or on the sandier and lonelier shores of "unspoilt" islands such as Ischia or Procida, or more distant Ponza. Such solitary visitors were, by then, a dwindling phenomenon. Mass tourism was beginning its long march. Permissiveness, for its part, would soon become a global imperative.

In 1948, when Graham Greene was taking possession of Il Rosaio, W. H. Auden and his companion Chester Kallman arrived on the neighbouring island of Ischia—forerunners in a movement to which the Ischitani would soon become accustomed. Far larger than Capri, and in those years far less worldly, Ischia offered readily accessible beaches, and the expansiveness of a handsome, hilly, countryside formed by extinct volcanoes—hospitable, as it proved, to new modern roads and cars, and to intensive building, in contrast to Capri's limestone cliffs and dramatic mountain. Though lying close to the mainland, Ischia, which had been appropriated in the eighteenth century as a royal hunting ground for the Neapolitan Bourbons, had figured little in the memoirs of past travellers. The very name of Ischia (possibly a corruption of Pithecusa, as the Greeks from Euboea called the colony founded there in the seventh century before Christ) was scarcely known outside Italy in the postwar years, unless to archaeologists aware of the island's antiquities, or to frequenters of her therapeutic muds and springs.

In 1957, as Auden left a changing Ischia for return to transalpine chill, he described the impulse that had generated a last brief collective fling of Anglophone talents on Neapolitan shores:

> *Out of a gothic north, the pallid children*
> *Of a potato, beer-or-whisky*
> *Guilt culture, we behave like our fathers and come*
> *Southward into a sunburnt otherwhere*
>
> *Of vineyards, baroque, la bella figura,*
> *To these feminine townships where men*
> *Are males . . .*
>
> > *Some believing amore*
> *Is better down South and much cheaper*
> *(Which is doubtful), some persuaded exposure*
> *To strong sunlight is lethal to germs*
>
> *(Which is patently false) and others, like me,*
> *In middle-age hoping to twig from*
> *What we are not what we might be next, a question*
> *The South seems never to raise . . .*

For Graham Greene, those were irrelevant considerations—his concern with nature, antiquity, architecture, visual art, sunbathing, contemplation, and even germs being notably circumscribed. Nor did he see himself—unmistakably and ineradicably English though he, as much as Auden, was—as a protagonist in regional contrasts. As to *amore*, he would bring that with him. Abrupt purchase of the Rosaio had presumably been prompted by the deepening love affair with Catherine Walston and by Graham's desire to be "away" with her in an exotically private setting, remote from husband, children, bad weather, and all the shared associations of England: to be with her, and with his work. There was little inclination, on Graham's part, toward expatriation or metamorphosis. Greeneland, like *amore*, travelled with him.

In youth, Graham had journeyed to far and lawless places, of which he had written with stark originality. Concentrated work on his books had always been done in England. In 1948, in a published correspondence with Elizabeth Bowen and V. S. Pritchett, he had given his view:

> Another danger [to the writer's fluency] is that privilege separates, and we can't afford to live away from the source of our writing, in however comfortable an exile. I am one of those who find it extraordinarily difficult to write away from England (I had to do so at one time during the war), and I dread the thought of being exiled from home.

In the same year, Graham bought the Rosaio, without intention of settling in Italy at any length. The house, with its vaunted equipment, was acquired—if I recall Graham's account—with funds blocked in Europe, perhaps from royalties connected with *The Third Man*. At the time, it was almost impossible for a private person to take money out of Britain, while any sum brought into

England from overseas was subject to annihilating tax. In his biography of Norman Douglas, Mark Holloway states that, in 1948, Graham Greene

> was to write the script [of a film of Douglas's *South Wind*, for Italian Lux Films], and for convenience came over to the island and bought Rosaio, that charming little house in Anacapri which Cerio, Compton Mackenzie and Francis Brett Young had all lived and worked in.

Holloway goes on to relate that Douglas, elderly and frail, grumbled about making the trip up to Anacapri—from Macpherson's house in Capri, in secluded Via Tuoro—for repeated discussions of the script. Since Douglas and Greene went on, however, to become firm friends and—as Islay Lyons's photographs suggest—congenial drinking companions, the association probably contributed to the lasting connection that Graham formed with the island. The film, like many of its phantasmal brethren, apparently dissolved.

In the event, "writing away from England" seemed to cause Graham no special difficulty. In the case of Capri, that may have been due to the relative brevity of his visits and to his detachment not only from the island's life but also from the altered England of later years. Place itself had greatly changed, and had lost much of its hold on him, unless as stimulus or diversion. Beyond all that, there was the decline in expectations from the Muse. The inspired pain of the earlier fiction would not recur; or even the intensity of those lighter and livelier works that Graham had once differentiated as "entertainments." What remained was professionalism: a unique view and tone, a practised, topical narrative that held the interest and forced the pace of the reader. Poignancy was largely subsumed into world-weariness, resurfacing in spasms of authenticity. In the late work, sheer human sympathy makes an obligatory guest appearance, like an ageing celebrity briefly brought on stage. When from time to time Graham told us, "I have a book coming out," he would occasionally add, "Not a specially good one." With all this, there were, even so, high points and renewals. In 1973, after receiving a copy of *The Honorary Consul,* we cabled to tell him of our pleasure in the book—one of the most compelling of the later novels; and he wrote in reply:

I can't tell you how pleased I was that you liked *The Honorary Consul.* I do think it's quite good myself but your praise warmed my heart. I am sorry that you and Francis are not on the list of Nixon's Enemies and you will be jealous of me because apparently I am on Colonel Gadaffi's cultural black list with D. H. Lawrence and curiously enough Henry James.

Graham completed substantial portions of his books during visits to Capri. On the evening of 18 October 1978, in a short, graceful speech accepting honorary citizenship from the municipality of Anacapri, he told an invited audience in the baroque church of San Michele that, at the Rosaio, "in four weeks I do the work of six months elsewhere." Capri itself, however, was never an immediate source for his fiction and is hardly touched on in his memoirs. Giving scant attention to the affairs of the island and its populace, he was still less concerned with the phenomenon of living in Italy. The courtesy and obligingness of most Italians were largely taken

Norman Douglas at the restaurant Le Grotelle, c. 1949

Visiting Norman Douglas: Graham Greene, Catherine Walston, and Kenneth Macpherson at Villa Tuoro, c. 1951

Il Rosaio (GIOVANNA LALATTA)

Harold Acton at Positano, 1981 (CARLO KNIGHT)

Francis Steegmuller, Shirley Hazzard, Graham Greene, and Yvonne Cloetta at Il Rosaio, 1979 (LAETITIA CERIO)

Villa Jovis (PUBBLI AER FOTO)

Casa Malaparte
(VI.MAR. DI SCALOGNA)

Léonide Massine's Isola Lunga

(ANDREA DE LUCA EDIZIONI)

Francis Steegmuller and Shirley Hazzard at Villa Fersen, 1977 (EVAN CORNOG)

Graham Greene at Gemma, 1987

(PIETRO QUIRICO)

for granted—but these, too, contributed to the ease and freedom within which he worked.

The ancient city of Naples, across the bay, never drew Graham's interest; and would have been viewed as a teeming potential distraction. He learned no Italian: "Never having managed French in all these years, I thought it useless to start on another language." He read fluently in French, but read Italian in translation only. He had learned to give "Capri" its correct emphasis, on the first syllable. (The mispronunciation "Capree" presumably derives from the once popular song about "The Isle of Capree," whose tune still brays forth from souvenir stalls around the bay.) If he had ever learnt of the old dialect name, "Crapa," by which the island was once known to its inhabitants, I think we would have heard about it.

Cyril Connolly, a contemporary of Graham's youthful literary life in London, sought to distinguish

> between the flight of the expatriate which is an essential desire for simplification . . . and the brisker trajectory of the travel addict, trying not to find but to lose himself in the intoxication of motion.

I think that Graham had at one time been impelled by both those urges, and, more darkly, by his wish to test the dangerous margins of his world; but that addiction and intoxication had, with age, been diluted by indifference. The round-trip ticket of the jet era, in making the travel trajectory dramatically brisker, had eroded those elements of risk and rigour that once sent Graham on lonely journeys to enigmatic places. What had previously gone unperceived and unreported was becoming the shared province of group travel. Graham's trips—to Central and Latin America, to central and South Africa, to Russia—grew systematic, prompted in the 1950s by a need to exchange one kind of unhappiness for another; and, later, by the lure of political ferment and of themes for a new book. All was interspersed with the odd yet unfailing return to Capri.

At the Rosaio, the rhythm of Graham's days scarcely varied: at work in his studio in the morning; in late afternoon, a walk, perhaps, with Yvonne along the half-hour path called the Mígliera, which, passing through Anacaprese countryside, ends in a spectacular drop of limestone cliffs at the western tip of the island. At evening, down by bus to the town of Capri for a drink in the piazza and the accustomed dinner at Gemma. The islanders, if they recognised him, were discreet, as were most tourists—respecting his privacy, possibly sensing his aloofness not only from undesired attention but from the ambience itself. Official attempts to claim him as a votary, in Capri's artistic tradition, foundered on that detachment: he was never a local phenomenon, an intimate of the place and its community. Visibly present on Capri, he had no air of belonging.

None of which hindered Graham from pronouncing, from time to time, on what he conceived to be the island's social and political moods.

In the late 1970s, Francis and I were approached by Raffaele Vacca, a member of Anacapri's municipal council, regarding the community's wish to offer honorary citizenship to Graham Greene. Vacca, the author of this genial suggestion, asked if we would forward the idea for Graham's consideration; and this we succinctly did, emphasising that we were merely conveying a message—but aware that Graham, soon to reach Capri, would not lose this opportunity of punishing the messenger who brought the good news.

Graham, arriving, immediately and outrageously berated us for "involving" him in community affairs. This was utterly unreasonable, and we said so. Francis told him, "Since you feel this way, I can't see why you don't just say no." It was clear that Graham would accept his honorary citizenship after extracting as much mayhem as possible from the prospect. The ceremony—held, at Graham's request, at evening in the eighteenth-century church of San Michele, not far from the Rosaio, without press or publicity and in the presence of an invited audience—was simple, dignified, sincere. Graham ceased grumbling, made his fine little speech, and was glad. A plaque, placed on the Rosaio wall, after Graham's death, by the Axel Munthe Foundation and others, was removed at the insistence of neighbors.

Among the multiple causes of Graham's disconnection from Italian scenes one might count his unconcern with aesthetic pleasures important to many who visit the peninsula. Evelyn Waugh, who, in the aftermath of the Second World War, regretted having neglected Europe during his youthful travels of the 1920s and '30s, later wrote that restless young British writers of his generation had deludedly imagined that

> Europe could wait. There would be time for Europe ...
> These were the years when Mr. Peter Fleming went to the
> Gobi Desert, Mr. Graham Greene to the Liberian hinterland;
> Robert Byron ... to the ruins of Persia. We turned our back

on civilisation. Had we known, we might have lingered . . .
Had we known that all that seeming-solid, patiently built,
gorgeously ornamented structure of Western life was to melt
overnight like an ice castle . . . Instead, we set off on our various stern roads; I to the Tropics and the Arctic . . . At that
time it seemed an ordeal, an initiation to manhood.

There were exceptions to this literary doctrine—among them,
the eighteen-year-old Patrick Leigh Fermor setting out, in 1933,
on his immortal walk from Rotterdam to Constantinople.

Waugh's regrets for unexperienced revelations of Europe's cultural twilight between the wars were not necessarily shared by
Graham Greene. Closer to Waugh than to any other writer of his
time, Graham told us that he "had never had the slightest trouble"
with Waugh's intermittently savage temperament. (An early biographer of Waugh, Christopher Sykes, sheds light on that standoff:
"I often saw them together and, due doubtless to the formidable
personality of the other, as formidable as his own, I never saw
Evelyn misbehave in [Greene's] presence.") Although Greene and
Waugh were close contemporaries, Graham deferred to Waugh as
to an elder and greater writer. His letters to Waugh weirdly verge,
at times, on the reverential.

Once, discussing with enthusiasm Martin Stannard's later biography of Waugh, Graham said, "I'm astonished at what a bad soldier Evelyn was." His admiration for Waugh's satirical novels never
faltered.

While the beauty of women inflamed and antagonised Graham
for most of his life, impressions of works of art, or of the ancient
monuments and towns of Europe, had little place in his talk or

writing. ("Florence bored me"; "Nothing to distract me in Rome"—so Norman Sherry quotes from the love letters to Catherine.) If, in this, too, there was the inveterate unwillingness to be prompted by received opinion, there was also lack of interest. As in many matters, Graham could surprise—by abrupt observation of some bizarre detail of his immediate surroundings, or by mention of some fine sight glimpsed long ago. Once in a while he would echo, as if dutifully, classic comments on the light and colours of Capri; but natural beauty had erratic claim, only, on his attention. In his Asian years, he had written poignantly of Indochinese street scenes—their languor, and their busy exoticism. The paddies and deltas of Vietnam could sporadically hold his writer's eye as pastoral England had never done. But he almost never spoke to us of a painting or a painter, a piece of music, a composer. To have suggested that he visit a museum, attend an exhibition or a concert, was unthinkable. If he did spontaneously make such departures, they went unmentioned. Our own pleasures of that kind—in the circumstances, rarely touched on—roused no enquiry.

Capri was an unlikely—one might say, a resplendent—setting for a man largely unmoved by visual experience.

Graham's generation in Britain has been charged with philistine insensibility to visual pleasure. (Waugh himself "sadly confided"—to his friend Anne Fleming—"that he got no pleasure from natural beauty.") Visual response had not been absent from Graham's early life; and some interest in pictures apparently revived during the first years with Catherine Walston, who had gradually acquired during her marriage a collection of paintings. If these elements were ultimately excluded by Graham as distractions, one assumes that they had no compelling appeal.

Graham himself spoke, and has written in his memoirs, of a diminished sense of visual appreciation that, together with a more pervasive apathy, followed his adolescent breakdown and his treatment by Kenneth Richmond in the summer of 1921: "For years, after my analysis, I could take no aesthetic interest in any visual thing: staring at a sight that others assured me was beautiful I felt nothing." Something of that aloofness evidently lingered.

Richmond himself—by all reports a man of eccentric opinions and appearance—had strong feeling for the arts. His very peculiarities would have inspired Graham's trust. He was a spiritualist, a convinced medium, something of a Jungian, something of a Freudian, a psychoanalyst without conventional qualifications, doctrinal methods, or material ambitions. Possessed of preternatural sympathies, he gave, by Graham's account, inspired care to patients received into his London household. In itself, the release of confiding and the deliverance from school torments into an atmosphere of intelligence and kindness would, as Graham later assumed, have played a main part in his recovery. It was a crucial rescue, and by Graham tenderly remembered. Moreover, it was formative. It was Richmond, even then, who encouraged Graham to write for publication; and who introduced the sixteen-year-old boy to established writers and to editors who not only linked him to the publishing world but who also represented hope.

In the 1960s, Harold Acton told us that Graham had suffered a loss, a few years earlier, in the death of a psychiatrist—now identified by Norman Sherry as Eric Strauss of St. Bartholomew's Hospital—whom he had sporadically visited during the suicidal crises prompted by his love for Catherine Walston. (Harold: "It was the ever-revolving Catherine Wheel, you know. There was need to talk to a non-protagonist." Harold—a fellow Catholic—added, owlish: "I fear the Confessional has failed him there.") Counselling Graham against analysis, as a process liable to deplete his talent, Strauss for his part formed an attachment to the patient. As did we all.

When Graham, on several occasions, talked to us about his eighteenth- and nineteenth-century forebears—benign and bizarre, cruel and corrupt, profligate and impenitent—he remarked that, while he had been closely questioned by clinicians about his relations with his parents and his childhood experience, little curiosity had been shown in a vein of recurrent instability and melancholia manifest in his ancestry. Among his examples, he might have included—but did not—his kinsman Thomas Stevenson, a noted Scots inventor who, as recalled in a fine memorial essay by his son Robert Louis, embodied the family characteristics of temper and temperament. Describing his father's "emotional extremes," the son concludes: "Love, anger, and indignation shone through him and broke forth in imagery."

Graham's close feeling for Robert Louis Stevenson led him to high resentment against Stevenson's wife—in his view a predatory and destructive influence on Stevenson's short life. When Francis once protested that Mrs. S. herself, while an undoubted oddity, had had much to bear, Graham would have none of it: "No, no. She ran him to ground, and she ruled him. She got him out there"—to California and, later, to the South Seas—"and she"—unforgettable grappling gesture, hands outstretched across the table with fingers crooked—*"got the hooks in him."* Eyes wild, blue, unblinking.

❧

> "One's life is more formed, I sometimes think, by books
> than by human beings: it is out of books one learns about
> love and pain at second hand."

Norman Sherry tells us that at their first meeting Greene extracted from him a promise to travel to all places around the world visited by Greene himself in the course of his writing career. That had been Graham's original concept of the biography, before it was agreed that Sherry should tackle the whole story. Faithful to the bargain, Sherry heroically circled the globe, seeking out survivors from Greene's youthful experiences, confronting some of the same dangers, contracting certain of the same diseases, and—again, like Graham—nearly expiring in the fruitful process. Had Graham enjoined his biographer to read, rather, the countless thousands of books, celebrated or obscure, that fuelled his life, thought, and work, consoled and informed his passions, and caused him, as he said, "to want to write," that request would have been absurd, unfeasible, and entirely apposite.

Literature was the longest and most consistent pleasure of Graham's life. It was the element in which he best existed, providing him with the equilibrium of affinity and a lifeline to the rational as well as the fantastic. The tormented love affairs of adult years—and, supremely, the long passion for Lady Walston—brought him to the verge of insanity and suicide. It was in reading and writing that he enjoyed, from early childhood, a beneficent excitement and ground for development of his imagination and his gift: an influence contrasting with that of his undemonstrative parents. Our own best times with Graham usually arose from spontaneous shared pleasures of works and words—those of poets and novelists above all—that were central to his being and ours.

During the Second World War, an essay by Graham Greene on British dramatists appeared in a series of monographs by well-known writers on aspects of English literature: poetry, novels, histories, diaries, drama, philosophy. The essays were soon collected in a fine illustrated edition of rational dimensions (we had no premonition, then, of mastodontic coffee-table tomes), which I, as a schoolgirl, bought in 1946—smuggling it home to avoid trouble, since it had cost thirty-two shillings of saved pocket money, and the flourish of independence was bound to cause a fuss. Turning the pages now, with their clear print and smell of good paper, and their knotted threads drawn from a stitched spine, is to relive the hot morning in the bookshop, the teetering stacks on mahogany tables, the trip home on the ferry; and an ecstasy of reading that dazzled the eyes. Those pages exude, also, the mildewed and still Conradian Orient to which, within months, that book and others accompanied me—the essayists shedding, even yet, flecks of pressed flowers from a hillside in south China. The book's illustrations, glossless, some of them in faithful colour, were my introduction to the miniatures of Isaac Oliver, to portraits by Kneller and Sir Thomas Lawrence, theatre scenes by Zoffany; to Alexander Pope by Charles Jervas, a flaring G.B.S. by Augustus John, and Sargent's Byronic drawing, in charcoal, of the youthful Yeats.

The essays are by practitioners of the first rank—"creative writers," as they would be designated today. The wool of obsessive theory and deconstruction jargon had not yet been pulled over the reader's eyes and senses—although Elizabeth Bowen opens her contribution, on novelists, by quietly signalling the danger:

> Too much information about great novels may make us less spontaneous in our approach to them . . . It would be sad to regard as lecture-room subjects books that were meant to be part of life.

Immediacy is more drastically celebrated in Graham's chapter on the dramatists. In the Elizabethan pit,

> the frequenters of bear-baiting demanded vitality: men and women who had watched from their windows the awful ritual of the scaffold were ready for any depth of horror the playwright cared to measure.

Greene's essay seethes with the magic of the plays and a sense of fellowship with their authors. There is lucidity, knowledge, a vigorous rapture and mastery of the material, conveyed through Graham's remarkable ear and in his clear, original language:

> "Think, we had mothers," Troilus's bitter outburst is not poetry in any usually accepted meaning of the word—it is simply the right phrase at the right moment, a mathematical accuracy as if this astonishing man could measure his words against our nature in a balance sensitive to the fraction of a milligramme.

Similarly, Flaubert, at work on *Madame Bovary*:

Poetry is as precise as geometry.

Graham himself expresses a Flaubertian recoil from stately excess. "Those immense rhetorical sentences" of the classical emulations that immediately preceded the free Elizabethans "lie over the drama like the folds of a heavy toga, impeding movement." Conversely, in polished plays of the Restoration, "the monstrous wig, the elegant cane, the flutter of lace handkerchiefs disguise their speed and agility." Throughout the essay, there is the author's relish of the sensuality and "the huge enjoyment" of great and accurate expression, and of breathtaking quotations that sent the reader, for a lifetime, not to the explicators and interpreters, but to the works and the words:

> *if heart'ning Jove*
> *Had, from his hundred statues, bid us strike,*
> *And at the stroke click'd all his marble thumbs.*

One evening, when I spoke of pleasure in Graham's *Dramatists*, he said that he had completed the piece on board ship, in a wartime convoy circuitously moving, over weeks, towards West Africa—without reference books or light at night, and between turns at submarine and aircraft watch. (Extracts from Graham's journal of that voyage, which appear in his collection *In Search of a Character*, are also invoked in *Ways of Escape*, where he mentions discovery, in the ship's library, of a thriller by Michael Innes that prompted his own *Ministry of Fear*.) He told us that, in addition to a trunk of books reserved for his coming months in Africa, he had brought, for shipboard reading, several long works he had never previously opened; and that one of those was *War and Peace*.

"When I finished it, I felt, What's the use of ever writing again—since this has been done. The book was like some great tree, always in movement, always renewing itself."

Francis said, "Like the oak that Prince Andrei sees, twice, in the forest."

"Yes. Massive, but alive in detail. One thought, Well, why write again?—since this exists." Then, with curt, dismissive laugh: "Of course, I wouldn't feel that now."

Strange that Graham, who had read incessantly since childhood, should have come to Tolstoy only in his late thirties.

Walking home, F. and I spoke of the image of the tree, which had moved us both. I said, "It was perfect, and heartfelt. Yet he was compelled to undermine it."

Francis said, "Agreement can gall him as much as disagreement. He won't share himself at length, or without reserve. The link is formed, repeatedly, only to be severed. All the same, the fine image prevails."

Over our years of Capri meetings, I seldom made "notes" after conversations with Graham and Yvonne. An underlying intention to record changes the nature of things, blighting spontaneity and receptivity: an imposition, like a snapping of photographs. In our appointments diary I sometimes find hieroglyphic reference to the evenings at Gemma, a few words of recall. One remembers long and well, and without prompting, what is truly interesting—the moments that, pondered, shared, revived, become part of the inward legend. Once in a while, in my notebook, I wrote in more detail of an evening with Graham; and I find that these were mostly occasions when pleasure was turned—as it seemed, gratuitously—to pain. One transcribed the puzzle, attempting to elucidate.

Anne Fleming wrote of Evelyn Waugh: "He liked things to go wrong." There was a strong element of that in Graham—the inclination or compulsion to foment trouble, to shake up tameness and disturb the peace. Like Waugh, Graham was arbiter and inflicter: things should go wrong, but only on his terms. Never a comfortable attribute, the bent for trouble is a kind of testing that can play merry hell with friendship. In these matters, Graham could be— like another of his literary admirations, Baron Corvo—"so amazingly unreasonable."

In an essay on the writer Saki, who was also among his Edwardian affinities, Graham aligns himself with those who "are quick to hurt before they can be hurt first." Readiness to hurt even, or especially, those who were fond of him and wished him well, had become a reflex in Graham long before we knew him. His novel *The End of the Affair* is in part a discourse on that theme.

Malcolm Muggeridge, who knew Graham from youth and was well disposed towards him, observes in his memoirs that Greene

is a Jekyll and Hyde character, who has not succeeded in fusing the two sides of himself into any kind of harmony . . . I remember him saying to me once that he had to have a row with someone or other because rows were almost a physical necessity to him.

"Someone or other" is chilling. Not only while the row was in him, but thereafter, Graham often appeared indifferent to harm done, hurt inflicted, trust eroded. Trust itself was an unwanted claim on him, another infringement. Chaos relieved the monotony of outward order and the dichotomy of his inner contending selves. Evidence of the pain he caused gave reality to his own existence, restoring him to his "better" self. All this is acknowledged in his writings—as in *The Honorary Consul:*

> Do you know what he said to me once? It was as if he were angry—I do not know who with—he said, "I am not unhappy here, I am bored. Bored. If God would only give me a little pain."

In Graham's first novel, *The Man Within,* the central character—who is an early specimen of Greeneland's man on the run—taunts himself with self-awareness:

> He was, he knew, embarrassingly made up of two persons, the sentimental, bullying, desiring child and another more stern critic . . . Always while one part of him spoke, another part stood on one side and wondered, "Is this I who am speaking? Can I really exist like this?"

Graham would at times speak scathingly of his own youthful work—as, in late years, he would occasionally deprecate his new fiction. We seldom asked him to inscribe our copies of his books—although, one way and another, he wrote in a number of them over the years. One afternoon, looking along our Capri bookshelves, he pulled out Francis's copy of *The Man Within,* acquired in its year of publication, 1929. On the green flyleaf, around F.'s own bleached signature, he wrote in small, spidery hand:

> *For*
> *Francis Steegmuller*
> *affectionately*
> *this ghastly first effort.*
> *Capri. June 1977.*

Many readers would not, I think, agree to the ghastliness of that first published novel, with its consuming fears and its cool intelligence that defuses the overheated plot.

Noticing, on another raking of our Capri shelves, Leon Edel's volumes of Henry James's letters, Graham said that he, too, brought those books to Capri: "They make me want to write."

To write fiction is to learn to inhabit other skins, whether thinner or thicker than one's own. (Thus Auden, paraphrasing the Book of Revelation, pays tribute to the novelist who must *among the Just / Be just, among the Filthy filthy too.*) In his best work, Graham excelled at those acts of convinced imagination and irresolute morality. There was, also, an authorial distance that could make it hard to establish where his sympathies lay—in *Brighton Rock,* for instance—or whether sympathies were engaged at all, as in *The Quiet American,* where cynicism, scarcely stirred by sensuality, expresses itself in violence and displeasure. In *The End of the Affair,* the temperament of the narrator, Bendrix, is unsparingly close, in anger, wit, and struggle, to Graham's own—so faithfully drawn as to challenge the credibility of the character by seemingly improbable contrasts of mood: an accomplished exercise in self-knowledge.

I think that Graham was not simply "made up of two persons." Rather, that he gave rein to disparate states of mind as they successively possessed him, putting these to service in his work. Of his plots and characters, he might have said, with Anthony Trollope, "They have served me as safety-valves to deliver my soul." His aversion to synthesis—that inconsistency of opinion and conduct to which he held as if to a principle—may have stemmed in the first place from a chimerical nature and predilection for disguise. With years, however, it had come to prevail for its own sake as a mood of defiance, directed against the tedium of rational existence. If paradox and secrecy were strong in him, so was a strain of candour, a clear instinct for discerning and stating simple truth. No less disarming—in view of the tenacity with which he insisted on his particular private myths—was Graham's freedom from the stock pretensions of knowingness. I never heard him pronounce on a book he hadn't read, or invoke an influential name in order to impress. The common emblems of "importance"—social and public attention, an air of authority, the flaunting of "edge"— were not his forms of egoism.

Malcolm Muggeridge concludes the passage quoted earlier, on Graham's need for conflict, by stating: "All the same, Greene is a very loveable character." The assertion has perverse truth to it, not least because of Graham's own manifest engagement with the laocoön of his existence. The laocoöns of others, however, must defer to his.

❧

We were speaking of Dryden. The theme literally arose while we were at lunch outdoors near a cliff formation called the Arco Naturale and saw far below us a circle of dolphins breaking a smooth sea. Graham said, "The skaly herd." Whether or not dolphins have scales, the phrase couldn't be bettered. Lifelong admirer of Dryden, Graham was impressively familiar with the prolific plays and the critical writings. Francis said that he had always contrasted Dryden's self-consciousness, even in the ribald plays, with the large genius of the Elizabethans. And so they talked, as we sat under vines at the Grottelle, drinking the traditional yellow Capri wine that was still, in those years, sulphurous as retsina.

I knew only the grand "occasional" poems, such as the "Annus Mirabilis" from which Graham had quoted. I said that William Empson had cited, in a work of criticism, Samuel Johnson's observation that what was claimed by Augustus for the city of Rome— that he "had found Rome brick, and left it marble"—might figuratively be said of Dryden in respect to English literature.

Graham nodded. "Not necessarily a good thing, of course."

I remembered afterwards that I had first seen that aphorism quoted in Graham's *British Dramatists,* where it is presumably drawn from Empson's vague citation. We spoke then of Empson's youthful, extraordinary poems; and of his critical writings, enjoyed for originality, language, lack of bombast.

Francis remarked that it was the first time that "literary criticism" had come up with us. Graham pointed out that Empson was a poet: "Practising rather than prating." We mentioned other mid-century examples of good prose by good poets—Auden, in *The Dyer's Hand,* Eliot, Randall Jarrell. Some comments were made, far from favourable, about Deconstruction, which had begun, then, to cut its swath through the universities; and about the modern obsession with explication and analysis that blighted the singular experience of literature. Graham said that there had been phases of the kind before, though never, probably, on such a scale or with such implication of the larger vacancy.

Francis told him that Gibbon had identified the same phenomenon as a signal of Rome's decline. ("The name of Poet was almost forgotten; that of Orator was usurped by the sophists. A cloud of critics, of compilers, of commentators, darkened the face of learning, and the decline of genius was soon followed by the corruption of taste.") He asked whether Graham wasn't beleaguered by theorists and dissectors of his work.

"Well, they do get in touch. But Antibes is off the track, you know. And I'm often abroad. When I'm in London they sometimes find me. They're wounded people. I feel that one has to give them special attention, because of their huge disappointment. One has to be specially nice to them." And suddenly, explicitly to me: "As one is to Indians and women."

Later—*l'esprit de l'escalier*—I told Francis, "I might have asked, 'And are you especially nice to Indians and women?'"

F. said, "The remark is shocking, and so one falls silent. Of course, Graham counts on that."

I don't believe that Graham was racist; nor, when we knew him, was he anti-Semitic. He was not even anti-British, although his countrymen had been his foremost culprits. A resentment of women—of their hold on his life—would break out in him, smouldering from past fires. When need for an enemy was acute, he would lash out at whatever came handy, always with the exception of Yvonne. Some of the long antagonisms were, like his anti-Americanism, reasoned as well as subjective, and called for thought rather than mere indignation. The more general condition was unattractive, sometimes cruel; the target often transitory, even momentary. Terrors of the playground were, yet again, relieved by bitter sarcasm.

When—before its airing at his acceptance of the Jerusalem Prize in 1981—the accusation of anti-Semitism in his early work was first publicly raised against Graham, he spoke to us of it, saying, as he had said previously, that he reread his past work with reluctance but had taken up the book most in question, *The Confidential Agent,* to see if the accusation held water. "And yes, there is anti-Semitism in it. I don't believe I was anti-Semitic. I don't find it in myself, or in my past. But the thing was in the air, between the wars, an infection. Of course it would have been better not to fall for it at all. Many people didn't."

Such failures are not resolved. Those who had affection for Graham Greene had cause, at times, to bear in mind these words from *The Comedians:* "It was as though somebody I hated spoke from my mouth before I could silence him."

Accepting the Jerusalem Prize, Graham was obliged to deal with anti-Semitic strains in his prewar writing. Nevertheless, since the prize is awarded, every two years, "to an author who expresses the idea of the freedom of the individual in society," who will doubt that Graham Greene was, through his life's work, well qualified to receive it?

Graham quietly declined the Malaparte Prize, a literary award given annually, on Capri, under respectable auspices and accepted by numerous celebrated writers from around the world who are probably unaware of the viciously fascistic past of the writer Kurt Eric Suckert, who published under the name of Curzio Malaparte. In his years as Mussolini's most influential literary propagandist, Malaparte exalted fascist brutalities, urging Italians to "burn the libraries and disperse the families of the vile species of Intellectuals." His principal association with Capri is his long, Futuristic, scarcely habitable house built, by Mussolini's special permission, near sea level on a stretch of otherwise preserved Capri coast: an architectural phenomenon much admired by some, and deplored by others. Those who saw it first in postwar years will not easily dissociate it from the German blockhouses which then flanked it and which its form resembles. Malaparte, a consummate opportunist, turned Communist after the Allied victory in Italy. He died in 1957.

One afternoon, as we passed, by sea, the red, low-slung Casa Malaparte, Graham remarked, "I refused their Malaparte Prize."

"Can I ask why?"

"Because of Malaparte."

To explore Graham's irreconcilable moods is seemingly to question whether he possessed any coherent centre of personality and conviction. Julian Symons once asked, "Can somebody so much in love with doubt be truly said to hold any beliefs at all?"—going on to answer, affirmatively, his own rhetorical question by drawing on a passage from the letter of dedication with which Graham introduced his novel *A Burnt-Out Case:* "This is not a *roman à clef,* but an attempt to give dramatic expression to various types of belief, half-belief, and non-belief . . ."

Graham's lifelong preoccupation with the equivocations that beset all men and women, and his consciousness of his own contrariety, themselves supplied a cohesive factor that, transmuted in art, gave the novels their distinctive voice. His presence was similarly unified by awareness. His keenest insight, Greenely "modern," was always, like his best writing, intuitive of the long echo in human affairs. There is immemorial humanity in the disappointment that Scobie, in *The Heart of the Matter*, notes in himself over the confused sequence of telegrams intended to announce, first, the illness, and then the death, of his child. The earlier telegram, giving hope, was delivered last; and

> I was so muddled in my head, I thought, there's been a mistake. She must still be alive. For a moment until I realised what had happened, I was—disappointed. That was the terrible thing. I thought "now the anxiety begins, and the pain," but when I realised what had happened, then it was all right, she was dead, I could begin to forget her.

That phenomenon, of death, false hope, and repudiation, is evoked throughout literature. Tacitus calls it "the double bereavement." It is found in Shakespeare, and in Byron. In Conrad, it is a theme of *The Planter of Malata*. In Proust, it is again associated with a muddle of telegrams. Oscar Wilde, resurrecting the mythical Ernest from supposed extinction, elicits it from Miss Prism:

> After we had all been resigned to his loss, his sudden return seems to me peculiarly distressing.

In Graham's case, the observation was drawn from events of his own life; in particular, from a disordered announcement of his father's death. The ability to refresh innate perception with specific modernity was among his most attractive gifts, accurate and compassionate.

Certain large themes, absurd pretensions, paltry personalities causing huge harm did arouse Graham's indignation, moving him to solidarity with the afflicted. His resentments fuelled discernment. They also led him to tolerate, as lesser evils, some infamies not arising from great power. Antipathy to the American colossus prompted him—as Seneca wrote of the aged Hannibal—"to side with any king at war with Rome." None of this invalidated Graham's prescience concerning United States policies in Asia or Latin America; or his loathing and harassment of Papa Doc and Augusto Pinochet. It did undercut the respect of those who valued his judgment; but that, I think, would not have worried him. He did not greatly care to be relied on.

In 1980 and 1981, only Graham among prominent persons supported an unavailing appeal, on behalf of human rights, made by the United Nations staff to Kurt Waldheim, then the UN Secretary-General. The incident aroused Graham's curiosity about Waldheim's falsifications of his wartime past—which became apparent to Greene, as to others; and, in 1981, we exchanged letters on the subject. When we next met on Capri, Graham marvelled that exposure had not caught up with Waldheim long since. (That would have to wait until 1986, years after Waldheim's departure from the United Nations.) I said that the truth was clearly known to thousands, and throughout the political and diplomatic circle; yet no one came forward.

Graham said, "They all have so much on one another." He meant, in particular, Intelligence connections, which ever maintained their hold on his imagination, and in regard to which his assumptions have been abundantly vindicated. His own predilection for concealment and disguise, and for the clandestine underside of life—paradoxically made plain in his work—was shared with many educated Britons of his times. "I like to have a secret love affair, a hidden life, something to lie about," remarked the statesman Duff Cooper, speaking for a fair segment of his acquaintance—and for an inveterate tendency of humankind.

We were talking about France in wartime. Graham had asked Francis about his return to Paris during the late months of the war in Europe, when F. was serving with the Office of Strategic Services and subsequently working with Jean Monnet. Francis spoke of "euphoria, unreality, anguish" in liberated Paris, and of reunions with old friends: "Even the French were inarticulate with emotion." One of the cruellest phases of the war lay ahead, but "we let ourselves be hopeful, being in the city one had most feared never to see again." Filled with uniforms, the city nevertheless proposed a return to civilian life. Soon Francis would see other uniforms, those of prisoners repatriated from the death camps. Still wearing their desolating stripes, those spectres gathered in reception areas at stations and ambulance posts, and were fed at a mess—a scarcely converted café—where F. would sometimes go at evening to eat at the counter, "on the periphery of their silence."

In Paris there was hunger, heatlessness, courage, factionalism, the black market, the rancours of anticlimax. Old people and invalids succumbed to malnutrition and cold. Younger citizens pleaded in the streets with Allied soldiers for food, cough medicine, aspirin, ointment. Parisians continued to astonish. Calling one day at the Hôtel Palais d'Orsay (now incorporated in the Musée d'Orsay), where Francis and his first wife had stayed at length throughout the 1930s, F. was moved to find the same concierge and his assistant, in their well-worn formal clothes, coming from behind the desk to greet him—with, however, the unsought assurance that "Monsieur Steegmuller, your furniture is intact." Chests and chairs with which, in prewar years, the Steegmullers had gradually fitted out their accustomed rooms had been concealed from "the new occupants" since the fall of France in 1940; and Francis was welcome to visit these pieces in the lumber room whenever he chose.

Graham asked if Francis had considered writing a book on France under the Occupation, a subject on which, at that time, little had been published. F. said that the theme had often been suggested to him and always drew his interest, but that such a book, which would be a work of years and could never be comprehensive, should draw on a multiplicity of events attested by those who had lived through them: French men and women who had yet to tell their difficult story.

He said, "Yvonne, it's you who should speak of this, not I."

Yvonne told us that, when France fell, in June 1940, she had been a schoolgirl in a village in Britanny. On an overcast day of that fine spring, German troops were convoyed in a stream of lorries into the little town before the eyes of a local populace fearful of looting, rape, drunken violence, and vengeance festering from Germany's defeat in the First World War. At her uncle's insistence, Yvonne and her sister were concealed in the attic of their house. It was immediately clear, however, that the occupying soldiers were under strict orders to behave well—unless "provoked"—and that there would be no molestation of the local population.

The unexpected restraint of the young troops occupying the village encouraged families to accept them, and eventually to allow their daughters to go out with them. Relief on the part of the townsfolk was agreeable also to the lonely soldiers, glad of a vicarious share in family life. Seeing this measure of fraternization, Yvonne and her sister asked their uncle why he had been anxious to hide them in the attic; to which the uncle replied, "I suppose I was thinking of what we did in Germany in 1919."

In the summer of 1941, with the onslaught of Hitler's invasion of Russia, special trains carrying German troops to the east hurtled through northern France. Yvonne's mother, who was *chef de gare* at the local station, was on duty day and night, raising the boom for passage of the incessant trains, signalling and shunting to give them precedence. The cheerful soldiers waved to her and shouted cordial, if indecent, greetings in German; while the villagers lamented that such fine boys, many of them still adolescent, should be sacrificed in the barbaric regions to which they were travelling. It was as if forgotten that Hitler was actually invading Russia, as he had invaded France; and that Germany must now suffer the ferocious consequences.

❧

In the late 1960s, when we first knew Graham on Capri, opposition to the Vietnam War increasingly coloured intellectual life in the United States. At the ceremonial meeting, in May 1965, of the American Academy and Institute of Arts and Letters—an annual event of inductions and awards attended by members in all the arts and by a large invited public—the Academy's president, Lewis Mumford, had appealed against America's continued prosecution of the war. Speaking "on my own initiative . . . and as a private citizen," and invoking the humane traditions of the United States, Mumford called on the nation's President, Lyndon Johnson, to "halt the escalation of error and terror" of American policies in Vietnam. The doomed conflict in Asia was not, as yet, the symbol of folly and wanton violence that it would become to millions of Americans over the next few years. Although the audience was a relatively reflective one, opinions were emotional and divided. Those who found Mumford's address timely and honourable were at least matched, in numbers, by those expressing outrage, which frequently turned on Mumford's having used his position as president of the Academy to raise "political" matters. Mumford, who had lost his only son in the Second World War, had no doubt foreseen that classic response; discounting unseemliness in order to make his appeal for the populations of Southeast Asia and for "the lives and prospects of our own younger generation."

Mumford was denounced, as reported in the press, as "an emotionally disturbed fanatic," by certain members of the Academy. Within two or three years, when antiwar sentiment regarding Vietnam had become a majority opinion in the United States and around the world, some of those same figures would be in the ranks of protest. Most people reading that controversial speech today might, I imagine, wonder at the fury it aroused, and at the possibility of disagreeing with it.

From that day in 1965, America's war in Vietnam would continue for another ten years.

Graham, who had been elected to foreign honorary membership in the American Academy in 1961, had learnt of Mumford's speech and its aftermath; and had kept a mistrustful eye on the Academy's attitude to the war. In May 1970, he sent the following letter of resignation to George F. Kennan, who was then president of the institution:

Sir,

With regret I ask you to accept my resignation as an honorary foreign member of the American Academy–Institute of Arts and Letters. My reason—that the Academy has failed to take any position at all in relation to the undeclared war in Vietnam.

I have been in contact with all your foreign members in the hope of organising a mass resignation. A few have given me immediate support; two supported American action in Vietnam; a number considered that the war was not an affair with which a cultural body need concern itself; some were prepared to resign if a majority of honorary members were of the same opinion. I have small respect for those who wished to protect themselves by a majority opinion, and I disagree profoundly with the idea that the Academy is not concerned. I have tried to put myself in the position of a foreign honorary member of a German Academy of Arts and Letters at the time when Hitler was democratically elected Chancellor. Could I have continued to consider as an honour a membership conferred in happier days?

Elizabeth Bowen, one of Graham's oldest friends and a fellow honorary member of the American Academy, told us that she had received Graham's call for resignation but had not answered it. Visiting New York at that time, she remarked, "Almost every American writer I know speaks out against the war. Why open fire on one's friends?"

Not long afterwards, we saw Graham on Capri, and he—with the air of pleased excitement peculiar to his exercises in bedevilment—proposed to Francis that, as an American who opposed the Vietnam War, he should resign his own membership in the institution. Francis said, "I don't believe that's necessary, as yet." When Graham, spoiling for contest, harangued him on the theme, Francis told him, "Graham, stop needling me. If it reached that point, I wouldn't need your prompting."

We told Graham that Elizabeth had spoken of his letter. He laughed. "She never answered me."

Graham contended that the antiwar movement among America's young, having compelled Lyndon Johnson's withdrawal, had lost impetus when Nixon, "with his unerring instinct for human weakness, had taken the heat off the draft," thus enabling the war to grind on for years. He was impatient with religious exemptions sought by non-believers; scarcely less so with young Americans seeking haven abroad. If the United States government were confronted with tens of thousands of young men prepared to go to prison rather than fight in Asia, the war would soon be brought to an end. He found the self-engrossed lassitude of hippies and yippies, and the mass cult of the young, ominous and abject: "I would like to take a machine gun to the young."

In Rome that spring, Alberto Moravia had also maintained to us that unmanageably large numbers of potential conscripts willing to face prosecution and imprisonment would force Washington to conclude the war. Moravia said that the egotism of politicians could be countered only by numbers: "Such numbers would be an index of failure, and that's what politicians care about. If American casualties were currently in thousands, the war would soon be terminated." When Francis responded, "One can't wish for casualties," Moravia replied, "Let's say, if American casualties equalled those of the Vietnamese."

The irruption of Watergate stimulated Graham. Prominent support for Richard Nixon in much of the British press had him in ferment. On the last day of May 1974, he wrote to us from Antibes enclosing an article against "Nixon-haters" by a London columnist:

Certainly you have seen this piece absurd even for barrow-boy Bernard. It doesn't merit a reply in words, but haven't you some friend in Washington who would collaborate in a telegram?

The President has much appreciated the stand you have taken in the London Times of May 31 and he would like to invite you to be the guest of the government in Washington on June 15–22. During that week the President will be making an important statement off the record. A room has been booked for you at —— Hotel. Only if you are unable to be present please reply to ——, White House.

You can draft this much better than I can. My experience in life assures me that the big lie always comes off and the barrow-boy will turn up in Washington.

Our love to you both from rainy Antibes.

We had to point out the unlikelihood of Western Union's accepting such a hoax. It was still the era of telegrams as well as of anger, and telegraphers in Washington were presumably alert to presidential messages of the kind. Expressing solidarity to Graham, we enclosed a copy of a recent letter of our own sent to the same newspaper on the same subject and never published. Graham's stratagem was not our style.

When we first knew Graham, I was surprised by references in the press to his delight in practical jokes—since a person less disposed to clowning, or to taking his turn as "the fall guy" (one of GG's favoured expressions), could hardly be imagined. But Graham's pleasure in such jokes derived exclusively from spoofs practised by himself on others. A turning of tables, which is the nature of the practical joke, involves an unwitting victim, a wilful humiliater, and a betrayal of trust. In his memoirs, Graham gives examples of his taste for humour of the kind, in baffling episodes that make one wonder how he could waste his time and ingenuity, or take satisfaction, in them. He had a ready sense of self-absurdity, but would tolerate no hint of bullying directed against himself.

America was the one theme on which Graham would regularly badger Francis. If argument was in the air with Graham, I—as a woman, and more perturbable—might be singled out for provocation on a fine range of topics. But F. was accountable for the state of the Union and, at times, for America's very existence. Most of this was fairly playful—or perhaps F. kept it so, in the face of Graham's determination to rile.

The third of July, in the United States' bicentennial year, 1976, was the eve of Graham and Yvonne's departure for France, and we dined together to say goodbye. On previous evenings, Graham, chipping away at the American anniversary, had made much of the fact that, in 1754, George Washington, then a young British officer in North America, had surrendered unconditionally to the French at Fort Necessity, on the historic date of the Fourth of July. Graham told us that he had sent a letter to *The (London) Times* on this point, quoting Francis Parkman on the horrors attending Washington's defeat. When we sat down to dine on the third, Graham, wearing the bedevilment grin, at once lifted his glass.

GG: I want to propose a toast: *Down with George Washington.*
SH: I have a better toast. It's Francis's seventieth birthday.
FS (later): How can Graham be so SILLY?

Graham had brought with him *The Times* of 2 July, in which his letter had been published. (Francis sent a rejoinder; but the letter never appeared.) In this, as in other matters, Graham's humour had a keen edge: the snowball that conceals the stone.

He was suspicious of the word "fun"; and there were forms of pernicious folly presented as entertainment that angered him. On a day when mayhem at a football stadium was in the headlines, he denounced it as "the new violence." It was one of the first horrific episodes of the kind—taking place, I think, in Mexico. Graham said, "At school, games were forced on us as a healthy alternative to belligerence. Most games now *are* belligerence." He added, "I'm not against violence. What I can't stand is brutality posing as fun."

Several of Graham's friends from early years had gone through troubled relations with him—Graham not disliking his disruptive role. In most of his long associations, there were, I imagine, periods when his friends felt themselves heartily disliked. But complete rupture was rare, and exasperated affection common. Friendships that had lasted from his first years of literary struggle were, with their bloom of shared experience, important to him; and departures from those thinning ranks were noted losses.

There was an evening when, Graham and Yvonne having just returned to the island, we exchanged some news of the past winter. With slight ironic smile, Graham said that friends had died: "Old friends, but all younger than I." He would soon turn eighty. "One wonders more than ever when one's own number will come up. Like Wordsworth—

> *"Yet I, whose lids from infant slumber*
> *Were earlier raised, remain to hear*
> *A timid voice, that asks in whispers,*
> *'Who next will drop and disappear?'"*

He asked what I could remember of that poem, in which Wordsworth mourns the deaths, in close succession during the early 1830s, of a number of intimate friends, all poets. Between us, we managed, with some slips, to say the whole. When we reached the lines

> *Nor has the rolling year twice measured,*
> *From sign to sign, its steadfast course,*
> *Since every mortal power of Coleridge*
> *Was frozen at its marvellous source;*

> *The rapt One, of the godlike forehead,*
> *The heaven-eyed creature sleeps in earth;*
> *And Lamb, the frolic and the gentle,*
> *Has vanished from his lonely hearth—*

Francis asked that we repeat them, thinking of the attachment between Coleridge and Wordsworth, and the estrangement that followed. We went on, then—

> *Like clouds that rake the mountain-summits,*
> *Or waves that own no curbing hand,*
> *How fast has brother followed brother,*
> *From sunshine to the sunless land.*

Graham wondered why Wordsworth had chosen "sunshine" rather than "sunlight," which "would have run better." The poet had preferred the less expected word. He remarked that "fast" was a welcome word, and that Wordsworth himself, having turned eighty, had died immediately: "Whereas now they keep you on the rack." He added, "It's not so much the eighties that I fear. It's the nineties."

He asked whether I could remember a poem at sight. I told him that I had rarely "memorised" a poem, even at school, and had no "system"; that I remembered particular lines at once, being moved by them, and then might read the poem over, bear it in mind, say it aloud when I was alone. Then I might remember it always. That had been the case since childhood. In adolescence and in my early twenties, when I had much solitude whether circumstantial or inward, I was able to recall poems from a reading or two if they were not very long. There was nothing diligent in it. Recollection was spontaneous, easier than breathing. One remembered all manner of lines that captured ear and imagination. Where there was greatness, the words seemed inevitable, as if memory had been awaiting them.

For Graham, something of the same: memory, rather than memorising. He found that he added less and less with age, and rarely recalled lines of new poets, even if he liked their work: "I don't think one is so accessible to poems that come after one's own era." Sensations aroused by poetry were in any case private, intuitive, unaccountable. In the past, poetry had been a presence that cut across the generations and the classes. One never knew where it would turn up. Like mercy.

Graham was to feel again, poignantly, the sense of anachronistic loss when his brother Hugh, younger than he and the closest of his male contemporaries, died in the 1980s. At that time, he told Yvonne, "It should have been me."

❧

In the mid-1970s, Graham was at work for the first time on a Capri subject, his commemoration of the Dottoressa Moor—who, in

1975, while the book was in progress, died in Switzerland at the age of ninety. Presented as Elisabeth Moor's autobiography, *An Impossible Woman* is partly transcribed from interviews taped years earlier. Graham had inherited the idea, and much of the task, from Kenneth Macpherson, who conducted the interviews with the Dottoressa and arranged for their transcription. In her medical capacity, Elisabeth Moor had attended Norman Douglas in those last months when he lived under Macpherson's wing on the Tuoro hill. The links with postwar Capri—with Douglas, Macpherson, and now the Dottoressa—were being inexorably severed.

In preparing the volume of Elisabeth Moor's memories, Graham told us that he was adding certain of his own recollections and supplementing the Dottoressa's "omissions" with his versions of her presumed responses. In his Editor's Note to the published book, he acknowledges such adjustments, concluding: "Nor have I hesitated on occasion to insert memories which did not appear on the tapes because the right question was not asked." In an epilogue Graham also mentions having drawn on the Dottoressa for the character of Aunt Augusta in *Travels with My Aunt*.

Among her reminiscences of life on Capri, the Dottoressa had included recollections of Jacques d'Adelsward Fersen, a rich poet-aster who, styling himself Count Fersen, claimed descent—perhaps authentically—from that eighteenth-century Axel von Fersen romantically associated with the last years of Marie Antoinette. Reaching Capri from France in 1904, apparently in the aftermath of homosexual scandal, Jacques Fersen proclaimed himself a votary of the Emperor Tiberius. In order to inhabit Tiberian ground, he bought, through the intervention of Edwin Cerio, a windswept spur of the eastern height of Capri, where a limestone cliff falls three hundred metres to the sea below the ruined imperial palace that is called, by its ancient name, Villa Jovis—the domain of Jove; or, by the Capresi, simply "Tiberio."

On the summit of that steep natural fortress, in the first century A.D., Tiberius passed the last decade of his life in self-chosen exile, neglecting his vast imperial responsibilities but conserving his power at Rome through a system of couriers travelling by sea and land, and by means of messages transmitted to and received from the mainland by beacon and smoke signal and by flashes of light on metal. A rambling pile, now, of roofless rooms and disrupted promenades long since despoiled of decoration (and, at this writing, shamelessly unkempt), Villa Jovis still crowns, dramatically, its half-circle of sheer escarpments encompassing a drop known as the Salto di Tiberio—the Tiberian Leap, where, according to Suetonius, those who had displeased, or overpleased, the emperor were flung down to their deaths.

The ornate new house created by Fersen a century ago, on his outcropping below Villa Jovis, was given the name Villa Lysis, in homage to a boy whom Socrates interrogated on the nature of human affections. The main entrance, in a columned portico where marble steps descend to the garden, carries in Latin the inscription "Sacred to Love and Pain." Fersen's practices there, his relations with other well-to-do foreigners then residing on Capri, and his death— a presumed suicide—at forty-five supply, in faithful if excessive detail, the theme of Compton Mackenzie's ironic *roman à clef*, *Vestal Fire*, which traces expatriate squabbles and trisexual scandals on the island during the first quarter of the twentieth century. In a companion novel, *Extraordinary Women*, Mackenzie—himself undeclaredly bisexual—again drew closely from expatriate homosexual life on Capri at that time, and on the larger rapprochement of mutual exploitation between foreign residents and islanders. Both books—necessarily, then, without "explicitness" are now period pieces, of special interest to those who know Capri. Both are well observed and well written, and have their admirers.

First published in the 1920s, the two novels resulted in Mackenzie's banishment from Capri. The interdiction may have been due, in part, to fascist policies of that time. Mussolini had seized power in 1922; and the dictatorship, while confirming its hold with gangsterish brutalities at home, was concerned to make a show of discipline and "purity" abroad. The more immediate reason for Mackenzie's exclusion was the irreverence with which, in *Vestal Fire,* he had depicted, recognisably if under fictitious names, the Cerio brothers and other leading figures of the island community itself—persons with access to power who retaliated without compunction.

Mackenzie went on to write other books, and to inhabit other, colder islands. So far as I know, he never revisited Capri. He lived long on the island of Barra, in the Outer Hebrides; and died in 1972, in Edinburgh, at ninety. I do not know whether Graham Greene ever met him—one of many details that I wish I had asked. Graham of course had read the novels set on Capri, and much else of Mackenzie's prolific writings. The two Capri books came up in our talk from time to time, and perhaps had a bearing on Graham's handsome donation to a fund for restoration of the non-Catholic cemetery—a mossy segment of the island's main cemetery, where a number of Mackenzie's foremost protagonists are buried, in damp proximity and, one hopes, reconciled, on a terraced slope overlooking the bay.

Restoration of that decayed Cimitero Acattolico was begun on the initiative of a retired British Intelligence official, the late James Money, whose volume *Capri: Island of Pleasure* provides an idiosyncratic guide to the island's expatriate past. Money's arrival on the island, in 1973, was inspired by Mackenzie's pages— from which he himself, an eccentric of anachronistic stamp, might have issued, so entirely did he seem to belong to, and inhabit, Capri's Edwardian adventures. Although his association with Intelligence circles was intended to be secret, the Capresi, with meridional intuition, dubbed him *La Spia* almost from the hour of his arrival.

Villa Fersen—as Villa Lysis has long been known—still clings to the historic cliff, taking the full force of Capri's spectacular storms. After sixty years of disrepair and absentee ownership, the house was resold, restored, and reinhabited in the 1990s. At the time of Graham's work on the Dottoressa Moor, however, it was a near-ruin, scarcely touched since Fersen's death in 1923. Inexpressibly romantic in its solitude and decline, it was cared for by a custodial Caprese family who for years intrepidly occupied the kitchen quarters at the landward rear of the building, while the haunted drawing rooms, shedding stucco and gold leaf, teetered ever closer to the limestone brink. The damp garden, tended by the housekeeper, was ravishing: suitably overgrown, encroached on by a cloud of ferns, creepers, acanthus, agapanthus, amaryllis; shadowed by umbrella pine, and by cypress and ilex; lit from within by massed colours of fuchsia, hortensia, azalea, and all manner of trailing mauves, blues, and purples—wisteria and iris in spring, solanum and "stella d'Italia" in high summer; in autumn, plumbago and belladonna lilies. Geraniums were the size of shrubs, and of every red and coral gradation. The different jasmines flowered there, on walls and trellises, in relays throughout the year.

In September and October, crowds of wild cyclamen, small fragrant flower of Italian woods, sprang from crevices of the rockface in which the house is virtually framed. (Once, climbing up to gather them, I nearly slipped from the cliff: an instant of horror that stays vivid.) Fersen's in those years was a garden of mossy textures and dark dense greens, with impasto of luminous flowers: a place of birdsong and long silence; of green lizards and shadowy cats, and decadent Swinburnean beauty.

Francis and I were fairly often, then, at Villa Fersen, making a detour to visit it in the course of the longer, steeper walk to the ruins of Villa Jovis. One pulled the bell at the Fersen gate and asked for admittance. It was possible to wander through pale, disintegrating rooms, to climb the graceful stair to the upper floor, where bedrooms and a long terrace looked grandly on the bay. Gradually, with inroads of the elements, the upper rooms were shuttered and became inaccessible, portions of the terrace fell away, the stair itself grew dangerous, the ballroom developed long fissures, the airy ground floor showed strain. Glass tesserae dropped from mosaic decoration indoors and out, floors were powdered by fallen stucco, and holes at the far edge of a garden path terrifyingly revealed the emerald sea far below. We did continue to ring at the gate, greet the dark-eyed custodian and her beautiful daughter in the secluded landward kitchen, and make a cautious round of the garden by a path uneasily near the drop in order to peer into the *fumatorio,* a sizeable low-ceilinged room, half-sunk into rocky ground, furnished with a curve of divans, where Fersen had created an opium den in supposed emulation of a Roman nymphaeum. Subsequently, the ceiling of the den fell in, all but crushing the grotto-like décor, and adding to the eerie danger of the whole.

Ever since Fersen's death, his Capri years have provided material for writers of various nationalities and varying abilities. Graham, at work on the Dottoressa and her memoirs, told us that Fersen and his villa were featured in the Dottoressa's recollections; and proposed that we make the walk with him and Yvonne to visit the house, which he had never seen. Afterwards, we would resume the ascent to Villa Jovis and lunch together at a rustic trattoria then existing on the south flank of the Tiberian cliff, looking out to the Amalfi coast and the gulf of Salerno.

The thought of that day gives pleasure—for its interest, and extraordinary scenes; and as a day on which Graham's good spirits held up throughout. (If Graham didn't enjoy an outing, one was made to feel it, and to feel in some way culpable. We left it to him to propose such excursions, but that did not necessarily let one off the hook.)

We met in the piazza, Graham having completed "my three hundred and fifty words" for the day, and being ready for a dry martini. From there we set out, with the spaniel Sandy, for Via Tiberio. The path to Villa Jovis is a steady panoramic climb of an hour or more, exigent only on a hot day. Anacapri and the Monte Solaro lie at your back, the Bay of Naples to the left, with the Tiberian hill slowly asserting itself ahead. The digression to Fersen's house turns off among orchards and vineyards, concluding in a small grove of umbrella pines that leads upward to the gate of the villa. En route, there was much calling for Sandy, who, by then unleashed, rambled excitedly among vegetable plots and underbrush, unsettling cats from low walls, unable to believe his luck.

Graham was delighted with the villa—with its haunted strangeness, and its histrionic queerness authenticated by decay. What measure of beauty or of nature he perceived, one could not say, but effects and atmosphere were never lost on him. At that time, the ground floor could still be entered, and we looked round the high rooms in silence, Graham enjoying, with slight smile, the unimaginable. Outside, within a low, broken parapet, we skirted the house and the drop, and stared into the "smoking room," which pleased Graham most of all. The den was then dustily intact, its low-slung circle of divans proposing the vanished company of jaded oddities with their etiolated host.

Graham said, "When I came back to Capri after Saigon, the Dottoressa gave me a tin of opium she'd had from Fersen, unopened all those years. Very good it was, too. It provided several pipes, smoked in my London flat."

References to opium—or to Kim Philby—were never without bravado.

Francis remarked that Cocteau's depictions of his withdrawal from opium in the 1920s were cautionary.

GG: I was never an addict, which Cocteau was, I gather, for most of his life.

FS: He gave it up, and suffered. Resumed, and suffered. Those drawings are probably the best of his graphic work—so, in that instance, perhaps it evened out.

Graham would presumably have agreed with the poet Leopardi, whose proposed remedies against tedium were "sleep, opium, suffering. And this last is the strongest: for while a man suffers, he is not bored."

I remembered the glazed, sometimes stupefied, clerks and merchants in Chinese shops and offices. We had read Maurice Collis's *Foreign Mud,* and began then and there to talk of the East India Company and the Opium Wars—standing at the verge of the Tyrrhenian drop, looking into Fersen's ghostly room through cracked glass while Sandy snuffled round our feet.

When we left Villa Fersen and started the climb to Tiberio, Graham said, "We'd never have seen it but for you." Francis responded, "You'd have got here on your own," but Graham shook his head. He told us that on first visits to Capri he had "walked about the island a good bit. But it's years now since I was up at Tiberio. The first time I went up, they tried to put me on one of those donkeys."

Small donkeys, the *ciucci* that had immemorially borne the burdens of Capri, were provided for sightseers in the island's carless districts into relatively recent years, when they were replaced by small electric carts designed for steep and slender paths. For touristic purposes, and to give rides to children, a terminal pair of donkeys called Tiberio and Michelangelo—the *ciucci* often being named, there, for artists and emperors—were stationed, through summers of the 1970s, beside the fashionable terrace of the Quisisana Hotel, where their occasional indecencies, in amorous mood, enlivened the cocktail hour for wealthy patrons. Out of season, they led a less glamorous life, rented out to carry loads for masons and contractors. They had their moments of high life, even so. The photographer Horst told us that, arriving on the island in earlier years to take pictures of a fashionable American beauty, Mona Harrison Williams, in her villa above the port, he had been able to pile his equipment on to some minuscule Augustus or Leonardo.

Graham said that the attempt to mount him on a donkey was defeated by his height, which allowed him to bestride the narrow donkey with both feet resting on earth. In a second attempt, the saddle revolved as he put his foot in the stirrup, Graham and Caravaggio ending in close embrace on the ground.

The climb to Tiberio concludes with a few minutes' walk on a last calm elevation, an unencumbered path that introduces the ruins—which, massive, tawny, labyrinthine, are honeycombed into and over that eastern peak of the island. What remains of Tiberius' villa is a maze of Roman brick, reticulated wall, and undulant floors, all interspersed with passageways, grasses, and the yellow-flowering broom, and culminating in a series of grand constructions—huge arched chambers that had served as cisterns or storerooms. The remains of the imperial quarters—the rooms of habitation, the imperial baths, the loggia and terrace—reach to the edge of the drop. Alongside is the *ambulatio,* a columned walkway where the emperor paced alone to reflect on state matters, and on lives and deaths, defended by impregnable surroundings and encircled, as today, by some of the loveliest scenery on earth.

On that day, as often in those years, we were almost alone there. From a wooden table by the parapet, we looked out to Siren Land across the three-mile strait that divides Capri from the tip of the Sorrentine peninsula. We ourselves were overlooked by the ravaged Faro, a Roman watchtower and beacon stripped down by the centuries to brick—and, in recent years, harshly restored. We drank the sulphurous house wine, crumbled good bread, harangued by a mother cat who appeared on the rounded edge of the retaining wall and called up her kittens, contemptuous alike of the mortal drop below and of our starchy offerings of bread and spaghetti.

That homely little trattoria, of good pasta and uncertain hygiene, has long since disappeared, its rustic building becoming the ticket office for visitors to the ruins. On the pitted outer wall of the room then serving as the trattoria's kitchen, there remains a modern plaque quoting the poet Statius, who, favoured in first-century Rome, wrote loyally of his native Neapolitan shore— where many rich Romans enjoyed "the blend of Roman dignity and Greek indulgence." The plaque at Villa Jovis reminds the traveller that the ruined Faro once reassured benighted mariners by the flare of its tall beacon: reassurance needed even on the rough passage of the strait between Capri and the mainland, where one of the *bocche*—the "mouths" from the open sea—flows strongly into the Bay of Naples.

When the promontory facing us across the strait was under Greek dominion, a Doric temple dedicated to Athena stood there, renamed for Minerva in the second century before Christ, after power had passed from Greece to Rome. Statius is one of several Roman writers who allude to the sanctity of these narrows, where sailors poured into the sea a propitiatory libation to the goddess for a safe outward voyage, or in thanks for their return.

Graham wondered if anyone now read Statius. Finding that we did, he laughed: "What swank." A little news from the ancient world usually went, with Graham, a long way; but that day, in receptive mood, he asked about the life of Statius, and the writing. Francis said that he had an agreeable impression of the poet from his poems—only regretting that Statius was overpleased by an invitation to the Emperor Domitian's table; and, in the same vein, too much downcast at being passed over for the foremost literary prize of his time.

Graham asked: "Who won?"

(It isn't known.)

When we had reached coffee, and were looking out at the Amalfi coast and at the sunburnt Siren rocks—locally called Li Galli—that lie just off Positano, Graham asked us, "Do you think those islands are ever really green?"

This, again, was Browning, from his Sorrentine poem, "The Englishman in Italy"—

> *and there slumbered*
> *as greenly as ever*
> *Those isles of the siren, your Galli . . .*

We had seen them fleetingly topped with green once in a while—in a rainy spring, or during a mild wet winter—and doubted that things were different when Browning, writing in the 1840s, set his evocation of that coast and countryside in a "long hot dry autumn."

"Greenly," said Greene, "was needed for the line, then. Well, that's all right."

Isola Lunga, most prominent of the Galli isles, has the outline of a miniature Capri, and carries on its stony saddle a low-set house—at that time, white and plainly visible, on fair days, from the Tiberian end of Capri. In later years, that simple house would be extended, and there would be other construction alongside it. In the era of our walk to Tiberio with Yvonne and Graham, the little island still belonged to Léonide Massine, who first saw it in

1917 during the three months' trip, consequential for the arts, that he made to Italy with Picasso and Cocteau. (The story of the difficult acquisition of Isola Lunga and of Massine's long attachment to it has been told in an excellent biography of the dancer by the late Vicente García Márquez.) After Massine's death, in 1979, the island was bought by Rudolf Nureyev.

Graham remarked that "the place looks idyllic, but might be hell." Graham was inclined to suspect—in some moods, perhaps, to hope—that most idylls might be hell.

A few years earlier, Francis and I had visited Massine on his rock. Francis spoke of that expedition, undertaken when he was writing on Jean Cocteau and wanted to talk to Massine about his collaborations with Cocteau and, in particular, about the ballet *Parade,* on which Cocteau, Picasso, Massine, and Erik Satie had worked and wrangled in that year 1917—year of the Western Front and the Russian Revolution, which produced, also, this seminal work of *"Sur-réalism,"* as it was baptised, in a word of his invention, by Guillaume Apollinaire.

In the late 1960s, we were arriving in Italy from New York to spend some weeks on Capri completing manuscripts. Francis had made an appointment, by letter, with Massine to visit Isola Lunga, which is most easily reached by hired motorboat from Positano. We spent the preceding days at Ravello, on the height above Amalfi and within an hour's serpentine drive of Positano. Massine, by telephone, had confirmed day and time. Landing on the island at the appointed hour, Francis was told that Massine had gone to Naples for the day, and that an arrangement should now be made for two days later. Returning, exasperated, to Ravello, F. proposed that we take a hired boat from Positano to Capri on the redesignated day, stopping off at Isola Lunga on the way to see if Massine was really there.

The waters of that coast are very deep and, near Massine's rock, clear in levels of opaline colour. The little island, exposed alike to a blazing sun or to the gales and high seas of winter, was that morning in transparent light: one looked up to the crenellations of all the coast, and down the Gulf of Salerno as far as the Paestum shore. Our *gozzo* was tethered at the landing place, the boatman settled down to pass an hour or two, and we went up stony steps to the house. We had been invited for one o'clock—as we assumed, for lunch. Near the entrance to the house—in a low passage under a concrete beam and rather wet underfoot—a platoon of huge children bolted out at us, shrieking, and ran towards the sea. Recovering balance, we saw that there were two children only, and that they were very small. From an outdoor shower, a fair, statuesque young woman in bikini came, dripping, and spoke to us in German. *Spamponata,* as Italians say—a blown rose—and apparently the children's mother, she was living on the island with Massine and with her own mother. Greeting us with lifeless civility, she told Francis that Massine could not see him immediately, since "we are about to sit down to lunch." We were shown up, instead, to a sizeable room giving on to a terrace that looked towards Capri; and there we stayed, unfed and unsurprised. Francis observed: "Another of Cocteau's jokes."

The blue, Homeric view of Capri and of the mighty rocks off its southern drop atoned for all. From the terrace, overlooked by the pinnacles and pastel villages of the coast, and their ledges of lemon and vine like vast green ladders in the radiant day, the island was a pebble within immensity. The sun drove us indoors; but the room itself, with glassed doors open, was infused with its setting. An airy, elderly *salotto*, furnished with piano, upholstered chairs, small tables, a worn sofa, it had clearly been at one time cared for and comfortable. All now suffered from neglect and damp. The decline of a sea-girt house offers no phase of seedy charm. Salt destruction comes in quickly, bringing green mould and brown rust; a powdery corrosion of metal fittings, the rotting of good wood. A decaying house by the sea is without present or future. There is only a past, of whingeing doors, palsied windows, and memories damp to the touch.

We had left our things in the boat and had nothing to read. I went down to the landing shelf to placate the boatman—who had taken a swim and eaten his *merenda* brought from home, and who showed no astonishment at the delay. Delay, in that part of the world, is an established context. Soon after I came upstairs, Massine appeared, dressed in spotless open white shirt, cotton trousers, soundless espadrilles. He apologised for not offering lunch, observing that, as there had been meagre fare, we had missed nothing: *"Mieux vaut s'en passer."* We spoke, of course, of the romance of his island, and he told us of his plan, of many years, to construct a small theatre there, outdoors, on which a beginning had now been made. He sat down to speak of Cocteau.

T. S. Eliot once used, in praise of Massine, the word "inhuman." He had a creature quality, informed by astuteness but ultimately inaccessible. His body was itself paradoxical—small, compact, but charged with enlarging life; insinuating, *câlin*, yet forceful and utterly self-possessed. Symmetry was perfected in the fine head and compatible features—broad brow, short nose, full lips of a controlled mobility, slightly prominent ears; and the famously dark and deep-set eyes. I remembered a small gouache, by Picasso, that I had seen in a house near Avignon: Massine as Pulcinella, in 1920, parting crimson curtains to acknowledge applause: a figure, unmistakeable, suited to its dispassionate Cubist forms.

When we saw him on Isola Lunga, Massine, in his early seventies, seemed little marked by age. Memory was prompt and prolific; talk expressive, intelligent; manner, cordial, formal, courteous. One felt that he consulted his own preference in all things—as with the making and breaking of appointments—and that, with him, that had ever been the case. There was a moment, indelible. Francis had asked about the origins of innovations that, at the first performances of *Parade,* had provoked indignation—the audacious "one-step," and the angular "Cubist" movements, shocking to an audience nurtured on classical ballet. To illustrate his own responses, Massine was suddenly on his feet, by the open windows, in a series of steps, attitudes, gestures that culminated in a pose of abrupt, humorous intensity. His blue backdrop was sea and sky, and the monoliths of Capri.

When we got up to go, Massine invited us to see the work in progress on his outdoor theatre, where masons could be heard resuming their afternoon shift. Leaving the house, we passed small lower rooms where children wailed to an accompaniment of minor crashes and there was an emanation of weary disorder. In a legendary setting, Massine had managed to surround himself with the least exotic trappings of suburbia. From the kitchen, the fair girl gave us a dishevelled nod, a tired smile.

By four o'clock we were lunching, at a trattoria of indulgent timetable, on the waterfront of Capri.

Something of this was related by Francis to Graham and Yvonne. I think that Massine's "case," on his Italian island, was the opposite of Graham's on Capri. Greene came to Capri to be away; Massine to Isola Lunga because he loved the place. Graham demanded freedom from irrelevant tasks and interruptions; Massine's choice involved him in constant struggles with the elements, with the claims of a confined domesticity, and with clamorous incursions for maintenance and construction. Massine had chosen beauty, with its inexorable servitude; Greene, autonomy.

At Villa Jovis, we walked with Yvonne and Graham through the ruins, on a path that leads, with little diversion, to the headlong drop facing Naples. At our side, as we went, the rim of the island curved on vacancy. Graham agreed that the little church long since built on the culminating peak of the emperor's palace was "a snub that might have been avoided." (A few years later, the statue of the Madonna on its pedestal near the church was blown to smithereens by a bolt of Tiberian lightning; and replaced by a heftier bronze version with pertly modern features, provided with the *apotropaia* of a lightning conductor.) Graham asked Francis about his Catholic upbringing in Connecticut. To Francis's own question, as to whether he was still an observing Catholic, Graham responded, "I haven't been to Confession in over twenty years." He repeated a favourite evasion: "I consider myself a Catholic agnostic." He said that he continued to be criticised, in Catholic intellectual publications, for "unsound" interpretations of Church practice in his fiction. In a private audience, Pope Paul VI had reassured him: "He told me, 'Your books will always antagonise certain Catholics. That should not trouble you unduly.'" Graham did not, in fact, seem troubled on that score. We spoke, in the Domain of Jove, of the enigma of religion in the newly sceptical, and newly superstitious, world.

Graham was curious, among the Tiberian ruins, about the *ambulatio,* where the emperor had walked alone; and about the remains of a presumed observatory for watching the heavens and plotting the imperial horoscope. Tiberius' withdrawal to Capri, and his erratic governing of the Roman Empire from what was then remote isolation, inevitably engaged us all. "It was fear," said Graham. "He made himself impregnable."

Francis pointed out that, even so, there was the threat from within. For private conversation, Tiberius went up—as related by Tacitus—to the highest ground of his villa, the place where we were standing, in order not to be overheard or surprised. When the emperor's favourite, Sejanus, overreached his power, Tiberius despatched him to Rome, ostensibly as his honoured emissary, and sent sealed orders that he be put to death. We talked of Ben Jonson's play on that theme, *Sejanus: His Fall,* and of the scene in which the Roman Senate unseals "the huge long-worded letter from Capreae," which is read aloud in the presence of the horrified Sejanus.

Ben Jonson, whose reading of Tacitus inspired the play, had been obliged to imagine Tiberian Capri. One wonders how he pictured it. One wondered, that day as ever, what Graham saw—or what pleased him, rather, in all the extraordinary prospect. (Once, when we had been together to swim at the foot of the Faraglioni, and were returning after lunch by small boat to the Marina Grande, we looked up at that suspended avalanche of dolomitic ramparts, cloven grottoes, spires of teetering rock; and Graham had laughed and said, "You feel that it ought to have significance.

Something should be going on up there, some event in keeping with the scenery"—sentiments of many a Romantic who had, on Capri, infused emotion into stones.)

In the autumn of 1939, after the outbreak of war in Europe, Robert Penn Warren, standing at the parapet of Villa Jovis, had looked out helplessly at history—

> *There once, on that goat island, I,*
> *As dark fell, stood and stared where Europe stank—*

and threw a small stone, his protest, down to the sea:

> *I could do that much, after all.*

Returning to the town, Yvonne and Francis went down ahead with Sandy. Graham and I, following, spoke of the fascination of retribution, for which, he thought, Nemesis had now developed, in "detective fiction," a current literature of her own. I said that there had always been, in life and literature, the thrill of flight and pursuit, the exhilaration of getting away with something; Graham, that there was the excitement of sin itself; excitement in guilt and fear, even in being unmasked; and that these elements were active in most good writing. We talked about French nineteenth-century poets, modern masters of those themes. Graham returned to the irruption of detectives into the novel and, from Wilkie Collins, tracked retribution through Victorian and Edwardian literature. I said that almost all Dickens's fiction was marvellously retributive, much of Conrad's also. But I was hopelessly outclassed, Graham being encyclopaedic on the fiction of crime and concealment. He enjoyed the early policemen in their omniscience—Dickens's Inspector Bucket, wise, percipient, and relentless as God—but preferred the freelance sleuthing of Sherlock Holmes and his progeny; delighting in Arsène Lupin, *"gentleman cambrioleur,"* creation of Maurice Le Blanc, and fateful figure of Graham's early reading.

The theme suited our Tiberian day. The implacable emperor marked the island forever with his gigantic presence, Capri seeming, ever after, to gather sacred monsters and formidable personalities— Norman Douglas, for instance, or Graham himself—who are ultimately drawn into its fabled strangeness, making part of the myth. *"Grande personaggio,"* an Anacaprese remarked to me the other day, on the path near Graham's gate.

❧

Through the 1970s, Graham's self-imposed minimum of three hundred and fifty words a day ("I try to break off where it will be easier to resume") still produced, with revisions, a finished book every two years or so: a novel, a collection of stories; more rarely, a play or brief digression into non-fiction. Work, his life and lifeline, remained his most necessary and exacting pleasure. There were, also, with fair regularity, the films to which his fiction continued to give rise even in late years.

With exceptions—*The Third Man,* which was made directly from his screenplay, and *The Fallen Idol,* which was based on his story "The Basement Room"—films drawn from Graham's writing were generally unsatisfactory to him; and that was often due to flaws in the casting.

"Yes, Trevor Howard was very good [in *The Heart of the Matter*]. He was a friend, too, we drank together. But the girl was miscast, and it threw the whole thing out. The same with *Our Man in Havana*—I had fun with it, Noël Coward and I flew together to Jamaica, Alec Guinness was excellent. But, again, the miscasting of the girl."

Landing in Jamaica, Greene and Coward had been met by the powers making the film, who had with them a candidate for the female lead: "Somebody's friend. One's heart sank. The girl was not young enough, not girlish enough, had the wrong voice. She was worldly, hard. There was lunch at the hotel, where the girl was not present. When the casting came up, I said the girl didn't seem right. They realised that she'd made a poor impression at the airport: 'She was overwhelmed at meeting you both. She was shy.' At which Noël snorted, 'That tart SHY!' After that, things rather went to pieces."

In 1984, in New York, a wartime film based on one of Graham's short stories was shown in a revival series of 1940s films. To Francis's note commenting on our enjoyment of that obscure but gripping movie, Graham replied:

I am afraid I never saw *Went the Day Well*. It was made by my friend Cavalcanti from a short story which was called "The Lieutenant Died Last." As far as I can make out it didn't have a great deal in common with the short story which was published during the war. The quotation in the title escapes me. I don't know why, but I always assumed that it was something out of Shakespeare!

I do hope we shall see you and Shirley during the spring in Capri, but God knows! We both send our love to both of you.

In that film, as in the short story, war brings Greene-ish horror to an idyllic English village. A crucial scene involves pepper flung into a German officer's eyes.

Among the great actors, Ralph Richardson and Paul Scofield were particularly admired; Laurence Olivier particularly condemned. Graham's dislike—emphatic and undiscussable—of Olivier's acting probably owed something to his inborn resistance to prevalent opinion. Fascination with theatre and film did not, in Graham's case, spill over into stage talent. His walk-on part in François Truffaut's *La Nuit Américaine (Day for Night)* is almost endearingly unconvincing. (GG: "I had a row with the actress.") In a companion scene of the same film, a cat does far better.

Graham's aversion to being photographed was not only a resentment of journalistic exploitation but a distaste, reasonable enough, for being depicted inadvertently and without permission. We ourselves disliked intrusive snapshots that made it impossible to be natural. When, at Gemma, the flash of a summer camera exploded close to us, Graham shaded his face with a hand that trembled. Once only, at the Rosaio on his seventy-fifth birthday, we asked if we could take the last four pictures in an ancient little camera. Graham agreed, but grew restive after the first two. At Settanni, an old, good Capri restaurant, miraculously unchanged, a montage of photographs of postwar Capri personalities would draw his attention: "Then, even film stars had faces. Nowadays, everyone is a pro."

Like many of his generation, Graham was punctilious in promptly answering correspondence—which must have been, throughout his writing life, enormous. The bulk of his replies were dictated, and sent on disc or tape to England, where his sister

Elisabeth arranged for transcription and posting. His letters to us, handwritten or typed, were seldom more than a single page. They had his voice, and his liking for a clear sentence. The tone was never guarded. Despite a repudiation—in *A Burnt-Out Case*—of "the exaggeration mark," he used exclamation marks frequently. However, letters rarely gave rein to the emotion and sense of inward ferment palpable in his conversation and his presence. Particularly in later years, Graham may have felt, with Dr. Johnson: "It is now become so much the fashion to publish letters, that in order to avoid it, I put as little into mine as I can." As little, at any rate, of the deeply personal.

As years went on, Graham's handwriting required ever more concentration from his correspondents:

> Forgive a typewritten and dictated letter, but I have found that even one of my oldest friends Mario Soldati cant read my handwriting and spends weeks pondering on what he cant read.

In editing and adapting Elisabeth Moor's memoirs, Graham strayed into that Capri with which he had never concerned himself. (One cannot quite speak of "the real Capri," Capri having unrealities scarcely accessible to outsiders.) One would not usually associate Graham Greene with inadvertence. In writing fiction or criticism, his impressions, intuitions, and literary intelligence had sufficed to produce trains of inimitable imagination; and he was used to relying on them. The concept of scholarship, or of research, was temperamentally remote from him. He did not amass facts: a single small event might provide a measure of revelation, to be affirmed in words. Once formed, his views were resistant to change. He was antagonistic to contrary evidence.

The Dottoressa Moor and her high-handed oddity had contributed to the Aunt Augusta of Graham's *Travels with My Aunt.* She had also, I think, played Scheherazade to Graham's sultan, plying him with stories of Capri suited to his sense, and hers, of drama and absurdity—to his taste for the picaresque, and for the adventure of the single spirit challenging a hostile world. Like other women in Graham's life, she had sought to please; to relieve his boredom and sustain his affection. Hence, in Anacapri, the Thousand Nights and One. Her vitality and egotism come through, engagingly enough, in Graham's *Impossible Woman:* the early life in Vienna, the rattling off of travels and sexual encounters, and lightning love affairs; and the more credible of the medical experiences. The Dottoressa's account of the death, in agony, of her young son is excruciating. Her own survival of that tragedy was valiant. She retrieved some of her ebullience, only to be broken at last by the accidental death of her grandson.

When that ultimate blow fell on the Dottoressa, Graham suggested that she recount her memoirs, "as therapy." By then, perhaps, her mind was inconsistent. Her tales of Capri are often fictitious; at times, they are fanciful "firsthand" versions of well-known events that took place years before the Dottoressa knew the island. To enhance her own favourable—and, on occasion, unblushingly admirable—role, she was reckless with the good name of decent persons.

Kenneth Macpherson, who would have restored some truth, was dead. Graham accepted the hodgepodge without enquiry, impatient to send a new book to press. Neither Graham nor the

Dottoressa considered a possible response from the islanders—few of whom, in truth, would ever read *Una donna impossibile.*

Graham was annoyed by our own attitude to this book. Although we praised its lively qualities, the suggestion that even small corrections were in order for future printings angered him. After a few bad moments over dinner, we let that lapse forever. The following evening, however, he greeted us with exasperated smile: "And now I've had a letter from this Doctor Webber."

Giorgio Weber, who briefly intersects the story of Greene on Capri, was born on the island in 1894, and died at his daughter's home in Florida in 1990. He probably understood and loved Capri more, and more intelligently, than anyone in the past century. We knew him first in 1970; but had often seen him in previous years on the island's paths—a fine, tall figure, white-haired, greeted and venerated by the populace as visible evidence of a brave and extraordinary life. He has left an unpublished memoir, of which his letter to Graham Greene regarding the Dottoressa Moor should one day form a part.

Some years after writing to Graham, Weber—finding that we ourselves had reservations about that book—sent us a copy of his long letter, together with Graham's lengthy reply: a double portrait, one might say, of the Commendatore and Don Giovanni that could, in another context, have drawn Graham's interest.

Dear Mr. Greene,

I was born on Capri, grew up on Capri, and practised and was Health Officer there for a number of years until December 1929, when I left the island for political reasons and emigrated to the United States. Therefore, I was understandably very interested . . .

It had not occurred to Graham that the island's past would speak back: that an eyewitness might come forward not only to vindicate the maligned personalities of the Dottoressa's account, but to testify to salient events of 1905, or 1925. Graham knew the truth when he heard it; but he could not yield:

> *Dear Doctor Weber,*
>
> *Thank you very much for your long and most interesting letter which I shall preserve with a copy of an impossible woman. Of course, I quite realised that the old Dottoressa's memories were sometimes inaccurate and sometimes she imagined that she had been present when she had only heard of these events later . . .*

Of Evelyn Waugh, in an analogous case, Martin Stannard has observed: "Sanity depended on his being right." Such sanity is itself a form of aberration. Graham's response to Weber's unanswerable letter silenced, as intended, an inconvenience. (Weber wrote to us: "I was tempted to reply but then gave up, realising that he was too slippery for me.") Graham would have put Weber's letter away, and forgotten it: aware, as he did so, that it was irrefutable. With all his predilection for the unexpected, he would not have welcomed, among much else, Weber's illumination of the Dottoressa's account of Fersen's interment, or of that "small tin of opium which Fersen gave me I don't know why—a joke, a whim. That tin many years later I gave to Graham Greene . . ." Graham now learnt from Weber that

> by the time the Dottoressa settled in Anacapri in 1927, Count Fersen had been dead nearly four years.
>
> I ought to know because it was I who prepared his body for shipment to Rome for cremation.

Weber, who had forfeited his livelihood and risked his life by openly contesting fascism in Italy, would have read with irony the Dottoressa's assertion that, on Capri, "one had not noticed" the dictatorship. In fact, the island, being frequented by notable foreigners, was important to Mussolini as a showcase; and Mussolini himself had sent a crony, Marino Dusmet, to Capri as fascist *podestà*. The party secretary, Teodoro Pagano, a young Caprese hotel owner who had been Weber's schoolmate, was nominally the leading fascist official of the island; but it was Dusmet who, behind a social façade, made the squalid decisions and issued the grim commands, while Pagano was there, as Weber remarked, "to do the dirty work." Weber was driven into exile: "It was this that divided my life—two halves that could never be reconciled."

In the autumn of 1943, as Allied forces reached Neapolitan shores—where Weber himself would soon return as a medical officer with the United States Army—Dusmet disappeared, spirited away, it was said, to Mexico or California. A quarter-century later, just as unaccountably, he reappeared. Revisiting Italy with apparent immunity, he came regularly to Capri for some years. He and his American wife would dine near us at Gemma, reverentially greeted by certain older Capresi who stopped by his table—to reminisce, no doubt, about the good old days and to assure him that all had gone to hell on the island since his departure.

With his wartime disappearance, Dusmet had left Pagano to face the music. Dr. Weber, arriving on Capri at that time to an emotional welcome, learned that Pagano was a prisoner at Naples, awaiting judgment by the Allied Tribunal within the massive walls of Castel Capuano. Presenting the Allied authorities with the story of Dusmet's escape and Pagano's subordinate status, he obtained Pagano's conditional release.

Into his nineties, Giorgio Weber passed the Capri autumn at the Hotel Gatto Bianco, where he received, in the pretty garden, a succession of relatives, friends, historians, admirers. Among his visitors was his old schoolmate Teodoro Pagano, who came to recall their island childhood. Weber told us: "Such things occur when one is ninety. There are only three of us left from those schooldays. So here we sit, Pagano and I, exchanging our memories. With some lacunae, of course."

We asked him whether Pagano knew that Weber had obtained his release from Castel Capuano.

"He knows, yes."

"Has he ever mentioned it?"

Slight smile. "No."

Teodoro Pagano outlived Giorgio Weber by several years. He died at the age of 103, an obdurate fascist to the last.

❧

The Capri to which Graham Greene came in 1948, and which I first knew a few years later, had much in common with the island of

Giorgio Weber's birth; and even with that Capri visited, since the seventeenth century, by northern travellers drawn by its ancient fame, and by the romance of islands—this one within sight and reach of a mighty city that was itself a capital of civilisation. By 1701, Joseph Addison, arriving in Italy and lingering at Naples, "could not dispense with myself from making a little voyage to the Isle of Caprea." Landing there, he found the fertile expanse between Capri's mountainous extremities "cover'd with Vines, Figs, Oranges, Almonds, Olives, Myrtles, and Fields of Corn, which look extreamly fresh and beautiful, and make up the most delightful little Landskip imaginable"—a description corresponding to the view painted by the German artist Jacob Philipp Hackert in 1792; and much resembling the scene that greeted the traveller as late as 1960.

For Hackert, as for Addison ninety years earlier, the long ribbon of the so-called Phoenician Stair, uncoiling down the western face of Monte Solaro, would have been more significant than it appears today—being, then, the sole means of direct communication between Anacapri and the main port; and the arduous route by which the men, women, and children of Anacapri carried burdens up and down on their heads. Hewn from the rock by Greek settlers several centuries before Christ, and repaired by the Romans in the Augustan era, these eight hundred deep steps were superseded only in 1877 by the carriage road constructed between the towns. They were in daily use into the 1940s; and have been repaired, now, for their third millennium.

From Graham's editing of the Dottoressa Moor's memoirs, it is clear that he was unaware of the presence of those ancient stairs; since he applies their name, of "Phoenician Steps," to the modern stairway of rubble and cement that merely links the curves of the Anacapri road, leading eastward to quite another part of the island.

Today, despite a white rash of angular new houses, that aspect of Capri remains recognisably "fresh and beautiful," its erratic continuity confirmed in the pictorial record left by generations of artists. In the past, striking changes of "landskip" had mostly reflected the deforestation, and replanting, of Capri's woods, which—predominantly of ilex and pine—were periodically sacrificed to grazing or for fuel, or to unforeseen emergencies—such as the 1914–18 war, when Capri, all but bankrupted by the evaporation of tourism, found itself once more thrown back on natural resources.

The capacity of an island less than four miles long, with an area of five and a half square miles, to sustain the ever-increasing tourism of nearly three centuries is one of its mysteries. The Grand Tour of eighteenth-century "milords" brought many well-to-do Britons and their entourages to Naples following the revelation, in the 1730s and 1740s, of the buried Vesuvian cities of Herculaneum and Pompeii—that influx accompanied by a wave of painters and writers who, in making the Neapolitan scene familiar to the world, further stimulated travel to the famous bay. At first the object of an excursion from Naples, Capri began to attract visitors seeking lodgings for an extended stay; and the idea of wintering on Capri took hold not only with British families but with Russians, Germans, Scandinavians, and Americans, some of whom lived on the island at length—and died there, as attested by their tombs. In the late nineteenth century, and into the 1920s, fine houses were built, mostly for foreign "gentry," on the periphery of the Capri township. Comfortable hotels were constructed, and small pensioni; and in 1907 Rilke was already lamenting the blight of those "hideous impositions."

The winter of south Italy, with its short daylight and damp chill, was then the preferred season of visitors. Prosperous northerners, coming south, were glad of the relative mildness and shorter duration of the Mediterranean winter; of palms, umbrella pines, and camellias, and the regular surprise of warm, brilliant mornings. That measure of reprieve sufficed. There was as yet no inclination on the part of caparisoned and corseted women, or of their bewhiskered and waistcoated menfolk, to strip for terrace or beach life; nor, until the all-shattering explosion of the First World War, could a northern society founded on duty, piety, and seemliness readily adopt an existence of indolence, near-nudity, and egoistic hedonism.

Other compulsions caused foreigners to winter on Capri. Faith in curative properties of the southern climate—the same belief that sent the dying Keats to Rome—brought invalids to resorts near Naples. On Capri, the new hotels served in part as sanatoria for ambulatory tubercular patients. (The island's grandest hotel, the Quisisana—today vastly enlarged, and still the most luxurious on Capri—took its name from an Italian phrase meaning "Here, one is healed.") Still other travellers came to Capri in retreat from the disapproval of society: unwed lovers, homosexual partners, and, less commonly, couples of mixed race. And there were the solitaries, who stayed because they had come to love the place.

In the early years of the twentieth century, these seasonal residents made up a "colony" of between one and two hundred persons, while, in the course of a year, thousands of Cook's tourists and other trippers came to the island as daily visitors. Of the polyglot "colony," most were worldly, and solvent. Among the wealthy, there were members of Swedish royalty and of British and Russian aristocracy. From Germany, there were financiers and industrialists: for two of these—the banker Andreas and the armaments manufacturer Krupp—the passion for Capri was to end in tragedy and suicide.

The British, at one time preponderant, were subsequently outnumbered by the Germans. In the interim, it was the turn of the Russians, who increasingly wintered on Capri throughout the nineteenth century. In a letter of 1871, Turgenev told a friend that the island

> is a miracle, and not because of the marvellous Blue Grotto, but because the entire enchanted place is a virtual temple to the goddess of Nature, the incarnation of Beauty . . . I have made three visits to Capri, each for considerable time, and I tell you this: that the impression will remain with me until I die.

Prevalent on Capri among foreigners in the 1890s, these well-to-do Russians would soon be joined by unexpected numbers of their countrymen.

Following the aborted revolution of 1905, a stream of Russian intellectuals, reformers, insurgents, and Bolsheviks sought refuge in the West. Many came to Naples, where they formed a Russian enclave on a height above the town. Scores of them, nearly destitute, reached Capri, where Maxim Gorky had established himself in exile in 1906. Gorky became their protector; and, with proceeds from European editions of his books, rented a house and barracks for them near the Marina Piccola. The little island thus contained, for some years, two distinct Russias.

Writing to Fyodor Chaliapin in 1911, Gorky commented:

This place is full of Russians. Moreover, I am on bad terms with them, and they would miss no chance of a scandal, if only to needle me. In addition to the locals, we have weekly crowds of tourists from Russia, they arrive in herds, fifty at a time, a wild and vulgar lot.

In those years, Gorky received a succession of Russian artists and writers—among them Chaliapin and Ivan Bunin, whose novella "The Gentleman from San Francisco" is set on Capri. In 1908 and 1910, Lenin was Gorky's guest, to the consternation of the supposedly "secret" police sent from Rome to keep conspicuous watch over the revolutionaries.

The extended visits that Lenin made to Gorky in his handsome house overlooking the Marina Piccola have passed into that Capri legend where many mighty, and some monstrous, personalities have been subsumed. Into recent decades, there were islanders who keenly recalled Capri's "Russian" years; and, in particular, Lenin's presence in Via Mulo. In the 1970s, Francis would sometimes exchange Russian phrases with an aged Caprese who, as the daughter of Gorky's gardener, had been taught some Russian at Lenin's knee. (Lenin had given her the Russian expressions for "How much does it cost?," "We don't give discounts," and so on: looking ahead, accurately enough, to the child's future as a Capri shopkeeper.)

In its long tradition, the island was hospitable to all these strangers. In the Municipio, the politicians were devious and greedy; but the community at large accepted its foreign guests with tolerance and good manners, making possible the expatriate existence of those years. Beyond that, the Capresi provided the reality and continuity that sustained and sweetened the rootless life of outsiders. The populace pursued their rites and tasks, spoke their dialect, and went their way—glad of the measure of prosperity that flowed from visitors so long as significant lines were not crossed: to a large extent, incurious; in some matters, implacable.

In the social and political convulsion that, in Italy, followed the First World War, thought and polemics were devoted to Capri's future. In 1922, in the shadow of Mussolini's imminent seizure of power, a historic congress considered the island's soul in the modern world. In large part, but not entirely, the *Convegno del Paesaggio* was a Futurist event, attended by figures from the movement that had acted as an inspiration to fascism. Filippo Marinetti, as its star, weighed in against the banalities of Nature, heavily favoring the lightbulb over the moon. The presiding figure from the island's hierarchy was Edwin Cerio, who, in an unsigned introductory address, permitted himself to execrate "the Jewish banks that, having set themselves to strip the corpse of the late war, had fallen on Capri in the island's moment of utter demoralization and debilitation." At a different level, however, the *Convegno* aired essential questions, which—like most such gatherings—it did nothing to resolve. Its document, now republished by Capri's Libreria Conchiglia, remains a revelatory work in the island's written story.

What had most linked Capri's long past to the years of change that followed both world wars was the rural nature of the island's life. By the 1950s, Capri's modern prosperity was already astir, but there remained an old guard of those who worked the land and fished the surrounding sea; and even those by now owning, or employed in, hotels, restaurants, or shops could still turn their hand to earthy tasks. The Pucci-clad summer scene in the piazza was interspersed with the unselfconscious passage of purposeful women carrying baskets or demijohns on their heads, and of men pushing or hauling a laden cart. Into the 1970s, the fashionable clientele of the cafés could rise to applaud the bull periodically brought, on his rounds, to service the few cows remaining on the Tiberian hill—the jet set clamorously toasting him in Cinzano or spumante as he was led by the nose towards Villa Jovis. The hard labour of the old rustic life was, by then, undergoing change and reduction, much of it merciful. But nature still defined the island's presence, touching its particular magic with infinity.

In the 1960s and 1970s, however, Capri was entering another of its millennial mutations: in this instance, a reflection of accelerating change—economic, social, religious, political, ethical, aesthetic—convulsing Italy and Western Europe. Having for so long kept terrestrial and temperamental distance from the eventful world, the island was now becoming a microcosm of the contemporary condition, moving from immemorial, if fractured, continuity towards an assertive modernity. Here, too, there was the story of peoples in newly prosperous movement, of swelling numbers gathered in finite and increasingly urban space; of mariners deserting the sea and farmers leaving the land; of vaunted, attestable gains and silent, inestimable losses.

The old Capri community—of shy children, modest women, courtly males, and other scourges of an unenlightened age—

lingered in its elders, and in memories; spectrally present on mornings of late autumn, or on cold evenings of Rilkean stars.

Capri has been a lucky island. Safe from Vesuvian eruptions, narrowly spared the horrors of a world war that devastated Naples, protected—first by the German high command, and then by the Allies—as a rest and recreation center for officers, it nurtured, in postwar decades, an extraordinary prosperity in utter contrast to the destitution of the shattered city across the bay. ("We are their America," the Capresi said of their image in Neapolitan eyes.) Even in wartime, the officers' rest camp had provided commercial opportunities for local profiteers. To accommodate and exploit the surge of a new tourism arriving in haste and *en masse,* elemental change was set in motion. Fleets of new hydrofoils outpaced the old leisurely steamers, and the port was enlarged to admit fast, capacious ferries. Scarcity of fresh water, which had plagued the island throughout its history, was resolved—after scandalous and venal obstructions—by a pipeline laid from the mainland. In consequence, the classic domed and vaulted architecture, incorporating the cistern for rainwater, passed away, as families hardpressed for room converted that drained space into flat-roofed apartments. During Italy's *anni di piombo*—the "years of lead," in the 1970s and early 1980s, when the nation was torn by disaffection and by terrorism from Left and Right—Capri remained secure, accessible, its air and seas relatively unpolluted. At that time, speculation in property, encouraged by corruption, drove prices of even the simplest habitation to altitudes from which they have never descended. Avarice showed its fang; and there arrived from the mainland, along with fresh water, the taint of organised crime.

The colours of Capri were also changing. Summer fires, carelessly or criminally set, periodically scarred the mountain. Seasonal detritus occasionally blighted land and sea. Barrel-roofed houses plastered in the old ivory or buff *intonaco* turned white overnight. The patched and faded rose, or flaking Pompeiian red, the bleached blue of Italy's deep south now disappeared—along with the streaked green of outer and indoor mould that had, in the poorest habitations, created reeking humidity. There were few concessions to character or tradition: immemorial rot usually gave way not simply to comfort and cleanliness but to cubified chic. The lofty rooms of fine old houses were divided into profitable double storeys. Solitary cliffside walks fell into dangerous decay, while green sites considered sacrosanct were obliterated by new hotels.

The generations, too, were retinged. Older women no longer effaced themselves in black, or covered their heads in church. The young went unisex, in jeans. Many sons and daughters still entered a family business—a shop, hotel, or restaurant; but other young Capresi completed the rigorous *liceo,* and went on to study law, or medicine, or political economy, or computers, at mainland universities. Still others took courses in hotel management and tourism at a special school on the island. Fishing fleets with new equipment came, from Sardinia and elsewhere, to rake the regional waters. The last olive press on Capri fell into disuse: grapes and olives were sent, in autumn, to Sorrento to be pressed.

Late in the year, as boutiques and hotels close their shutters and the island recovers quietude, the exhausted Capresi—who once spent drear, arthritic winters repairing their houses and recaulking their boats—depart for spas and ski resorts, and for exotic holidays around the world. Families of ten or a dozen children, once common, are now a phenomenon of the past, and Capri's population is stabilized at about 12,000 souls—more than fourfold the numbers of a century ago. It is a population as widely travelled, these days, as most of the visitors who reach the island's shores.

Thinking of those times of transition—and of their violations, contested in vain and now institutionalised and extended—a lover of Capri must gratefully wonder that beauty continues to prevail there—not as touristic prettiness, but in the grand and ultimate indifference of Nature to the antics of humankind. In a future age, perhaps, even today's silliness may slide away, as have the courts of emperors, and the incursions of centuried invaders.

I don't remember that we ever discussed, with Graham and Yvonne, these transformations of island life. We were all conscious enough of uproar in far places, and one cannot be forever throwing up one's hands at the world's condition. To recount the forebodings of our Capresi friends, or catalogue official iniquities, would have been tedious. Graham's scant information on island matters was mostly gleaned from the family who tended his property. His other Capri connections were few, and he didn't seek to extend them. If, as he sat with Yvonne in the piazza before dinner, he saw us speaking with one of the islanders, he might later ask, "Who was that?" and want to know what we had talked about. Such moments were a flicker, only, of curiosity—into our own habits, perhaps, as much as those of the Capresi. The island had not "grown" on him: he came there, as much as ever, to be "away." At the Rosaio, he could still preserve his working day, with interruptions only of his choosing.

For us, arriving out of season and staying in a part of Capri where there are no cars, the island offered more than a ritual privacy for work. New evils and evildoers could scarcely now recast, for us, its daily adventure or storied continuity. Countless *gentilezze* and affinities had marked our years in that community: graces never intrusive, never impersonal. One had assisted at baptisms and weddings, one had paused for the tolling bell. There had been, as we chose, the liveliness of friendship, or the needful silence: stillness has ever lain at the heart of Capri's drama. Speaking to Graham of our lives in cities, I once remarked that a quality of silence had become unattainable. He exclaimed: "The meaningless, insistent noise—I find it intolerable. The world is a raucous radio held to one's ear." He said, "Silence is now the most expensive commodity on earth. If you were to go to the desert, a plane would roar over."

Francis said we were harassed by new noises—the invented intrusions of machines. Sounds in nature often made part of silence.

Graham laughed. "I like a storm."

The excitement of Capri's titanic storms—how we enjoyed them: at night, safe in our beds, shutters open on nearly continuous lightning, thunder reverberating from the rock face of the mountain and rumbling in innumerable grottoes while sheets of rain sluiced the windows. Neapolitan, Tiberian storms, dreaded by mariners, farmers, and the mainland poor; old-fashioned tempests that can still suspend coastal sea traffic for a couple of days, restoring to islands the illusion of an old solitude.

🦋

Graham was stoical about his health, merely remarking on infirmities of age or mentioning, "I had an operation." He spoke of suffocating tests on his lungs.

GG: They said I had lung cancer. That was a relief.
SH: Why?
GG: Because I knew I didn't have it.

In his early eighties, he seemed temperamentally unchanged. Bodily, he had never been robust—rather, there was the spindling tenacity that resisted age as it had resisted much else. The years showed in his "hurt, offended face," which at times seemed stricken with all that it had borne, entertained, relished, resented, and expressed. Although writing continued to be the core of life, he showed less and less satisfaction in the completion of a book, even when it was strong and well received. In 1978, he had written to us about *The Human Factor,* on which he had intermittently worked for years:

> I thought I had shifted the albatross off my neck, but now it lingers on mouldering slowly. How I hate the publicity which has surrounded this book unlike the others.

All subsequent books were short, and mentioned as if their publication had become burdensome. The discipline of daily work, however, never flagged.

During our years of meeting and corresponding, Graham, based at Antibes, had travelled constantly. Letters had been written on the eve of "six weeks in South Africa," or a trip to Panama, to Switzerland, to Spain; and once, on the quiet, to Washington. Journeys had often been politically as well as literarily motivated, and fraught with the sort of obstacles that engaged Graham's interest:

I am afraid that after all events made it impossible for me to go to Poland. It seemed to me that under the circumstances I would not have freedom of movement and in any case anyone to whom I spoke could come under suspicion from the authorities, so I decided not to go. WAYS OF ESCAPE unfortunately would probably have been read and it would have been noted that on my visit in the Fifties I had smuggled a gold watch to a potential dissenter and had also been asked to carry with me a tape recorder even though I didn't do so.

Now, in his eighties, Graham was writing—

A hasty line as I'm just back from Spain and preparing for Russia . . .

The indomitable need for movement took a toll, perhaps. There was still less repose when Graham found a subject close to home. In the early 1980s, he and Yvonne had been seized with the marital difficulties of Yvonne's daughter, Martine—an imbroglio that moved Graham to scrutinise organised crime along the Côte d'Azur. In the new year of 1982, he wrote to Francis:

I have launched an attack on the milieu of Nice which means that I am all day on the telephone or the parlaphone and seeing an average of four journalists a day which is certainly not my cup of tea . . . The fight now is really with the criminal milieu here and it occupies all my time.

That episode produced a brief polemical book, *J'Accuse.* An ensuing court action dragged on for many months, to an equivocal conclusion. The ebb and flow of these events consumed Graham's days, interrupting the rhythm of his Capri visits while he remained in France for attendance in the courts. When we did coincide on the island, he was exceptionally on edge, the need for an adversary not appeased by evils on what he called la Côte d'Ordure. There were times when almost any remark brought argument or flat contradiction. Coming away at the end of such an evening, I told Francis that one seemed to have strayed into the provincial debating society. (F. felt that, in our era, all debating societies are provincial.) One missed laughter, books, the conversational adventure; missed, I suppose, friendship.

If we stayed away, Graham would ask why we hadn't come. If we appeared as usual, he tended to hector. Often dispiriting, this was sometimes ludicrous.

In those years, at summer's end, abandoned cats and dogs wandered the island's paths in search of patronage. Like others, I fed animals who came our way, attracting smiles and stares. One evening, on our walk to Gemma, we were tracked by three little boys who followed us to the piazza with loud meowings and fits of giggles. We were smiling over this as we entered the restaurant— where one saw that Graham, having had, possibly, too calm a day, was spoiling for trouble. In my notebook I find the following:

GG (with blue glare): What are you laughing about?
F. explains that s. feeds cats, etc.—info that would not otherwise be volunteered.

GG (to me, in fury): You realise that you're only prolonging the agony.

SH: I suppose that's what they said to the Good Samaritan.

Pause.

GG (with angry, conceding laugh): Oh well—I suppose a human being is more important than an animal.

Yvonne was amused.

I remembered [from *The Heart of the Matter*]:

> "One may love a dog more than any other possession, but one wouldn't run down even a strange child to save it."

Later, FRANCIS: All I know is that we came into the restaurant laughing. Then laughed no more.

With Graham, a woman did not get good marks for pert answers. In the way of censorious persons, he bridled at the idea that he himself was judged, even in small matters. Amusement shown by women rankled at length. Like the people of Aragon in the *zarzuela,* he could not forget, change, or pretend.

There was a dinner at Laetitia Cerio's, with guests from abroad. For such evenings Graham wore, instead of his usual and casual clothes, a dark suit, white shirt, red tie. Formality became him. He arrived in sombre mood, drank a bit; at table, talked to the unknown guests; fell silent. One of the foreigners was from the American press, not a good choice with Graham. After dinner, he came to speak to me where I was standing, ready to leave. He started up with a contentious theme that I had avoided the evening before: I told him that we would not agree, and that such a discussion would only annoy him.

Graham flared into mindless rage. Those were the worst moments I ever had with him, irrational and cruel: paroxysm of the playground.

At that time, there still proliferated in south Italy the phenomenon of the *mozzo*—small boys who at all hours delivered notes, packages, flowers; who, more professionally, could be seen, in white jacket, nimbly carrying through traffic and crowds a thimbleful of espresso on a tiny tray. On the evening after our dinner at Laetitia's, Graham sent me a note, by hand of the *mozzo:*

> We hoped to see you tonight so that I could apologise for my evil temper last night. The truth is—I felt we had been hijacked by Laetitia (poor innocent!) for the journalist and his ghastly wife. I'm afraid I took it out on you!

Throughout those hearings in the French courts, Graham was under an unfamiliar strain. He had again embroiled himself in a need to marshal factual realities; and had necessarily exposed his private life at Antibes to press scrutiny. The case was long in the courts. He could not compel the desired result. More than most people, he did not care to be thwarted.

At the time of Graham's engagement with *J'Accuse,* Harold Acton came to Naples for a few days—an Anglo-Florentine who delighted in Neapolitan energies, and in the city's genial indifference to modern assumptions. In 1956, with *The Bourbons of Naples*—later extended by his companion volume on the last Bourbons—Harold had first brought the prodigious Neapolitan eighteenth century before a modern English-reading public. That history was complemented, in 1969, by Brian Fothergill's biography, *Sir William Hamilton,* which did revelatory justice to the remarkable man until then disregarded as merely the complaisant husband of the enchantress Emma.

Harold had made his name in early youth, as a writer but, above all, as a unique and brilliant presence who was, in Graham's words, "generous and fearless." As with Graham, we had known him only since his middle years—beginning in the early 1960s, when we were much at Florence and saw him frequently. A self-described aesthete, he was vigorous, tall, muscular, with powerful neck and shoulders. His expressive face was smooth into late age. He was almost completely bald. (During the youthful years in China, a Cantonese servant, noting his employer's loss of hair, had commented: "Soon all like face.") Harold came into a room rapidly, eagerly, with tripping schoolboy walk and with a balance of animation and equanimity that conveyed good humour and good manners. (It was said of him that he had never preceded anyone out of a room.) At Florence, he lived grandly, but without arrogance or wish for cachet. The renowned courtesy was itself the mark of imagination and kindness, and of close attention. He had no need to "win." In company, he could not see anybody excluded or humiliated.

Harold's subtlety of manner, often called "Mandarin," was probably formed before his years in China. His talk had a Western brilliance of vocabulary and wit, a prevailing openness to seriousness as well as to variety and absurdity. His literary pleasures were not widely different from Graham Greene's, though differently nurtured and expressed; and Harold, too, was immensely well-read.

But their temperaments were utterly contrasting. Harold was knowledgeable, curious, passionate about every form of art, and moved by natural beauty whether in humans or of the earth.

At Harold's death, in February 1994, Alan Pryce-Jones, who knew him a lifetime, wrote that even in early youth

> he displayed one unequalled gift: that of throwing into the air a stream of dazzling talk. In this field he was entirely his own man . . . an incomparable builder of cloud-castles, with at his command a wonderful range of verbal modulation, which wrung every last drop from his own cleverness.

That sonorous voice, at times nearly singsong, was the medium for a rich vocabulary in which "forthwith" or "withal" or "albeit" were boldly refreshed and brought into play; in which "slake" or "pullulate" would be splendidly deployed. Harold's enunciation of "writhe" or "wrest" made the *w,* and the contortion, palpable. All was unforced, unembarrassed, amusing and amused. There was no attempt to monopolise: he sought to stimulate the thought and talk of others, to bring the moments alive. Any signal of originality drew him to all manner of strangers, and bound him to friends. Peter Quennell has written that "Harold possessed the gift of raising the spirits, and electrifying the atmosphere, of any occasion he attended." From his company one brought away unique lightness, tolerance, a sense of joy.

Tragedy and loss had sharpened, perhaps, an intense sympathy for creativity.

Having read, in *More Memoirs,* Harold's brief account of being torpedoed in the Atlantic in 1942 (noting the calm fatalism of his comrades, he wondered whether one would "really relive one's whole life in the moment of drowning"), we had asked him about his grim war. I remarked that, on a lesser level, the years without privacy would themselves have been an ordeal; and he at once corrected me: "But I always met such interesting people!" He said, "Everyone was reading, reading. On troopships, in barracks, in hospital, all were reading. They were drafting poems, and sending them to *New Writing*." A fresh view, perhaps, of life under arms; but in fact John Lehmann's magazine during those years carried many poems from the fire zones of the world.

Harold had begun, in schooldays, precociously and even iconoclastically, with poetry and fiction. The early dream remained undeveloped. He was diffident about his achievement, saying that he would be known, "if at all," as historian and memoirist, and as a translator of Chinese plays. For his life and personality, he made no claims. Once, on discovering that we regularly visited Uberto Strozzi, a frail Florentine figure of infinite civilisation who lived reclusively as custodian of a deranged brother, Harold exclaimed, "If he is your friend, then you know the most interesting man in Florence." Francis said, "I think we know the two most interesting men in Florence."

At La Pietra, his great house on Via Bolognese, Harold was engrossed by visitors from abroad—friends, and the friends of friends; acquaintances, and their circle of acquaintance. To these he gave hospitality and unjaded attention, while the procession steadily consumed his writing time. We proposed only those of our own visitors who might truly interest him. One evening, we brought with us Ivan Morris, whose Japanese scholarship was much admired by Harold. Walking in the garden before dinner, we fell behind so that they might talk alone. Ivan told us afterwards that they had spoken at length of Arthur Waley—close to both men not only as transcendent Orientalist but as Harold's intimate friend since youth, and as Ivan's teacher at Oxford in postwar years. Ivan had asked if Harold could shed light on Waley's "failure" ever to visit China and Japan, the sources of his life's work. Harold: "Ooh yes. Arthur had a recurrent stoppage." In the first half of the twentieth century, a journey from Britain to the Far East required many weeks at sea, with uncertain access to medical care; and Waley, by Harold's account, had been obliged to stay close to home.

When, in the mid-1980s, Harold visited Naples, friends had arranged a quiet dinner by the Naples shore—where we arrived to find our quintet enlarged by the addition of a journalist from New York, who had apparently pleaded for inclusion. ("It's been the ambition of my life to meet Harold Acton. I've read every word he ever wrote.") At table, the newcomer took charge: compliments were pelted like confetti, questions plied without pause for answer. At length, arm raking the soft night, luminous bay, and looming Vesuvius, the journalist cried out: "I can't believe this. That I'm sitting here with the author of *Under the Volcano*."

The preposterous remark did not register with our Neapolitan hosts. Francis and I looked at the sea.

Harold replied instantly, with utter simplicity: "I did not write that book, which is the work of a great novelist. I'm honoured that you should associate me with it. It's one of the modern novels I most admire, as I admire everything that Malcolm Lowry wrote." Harold felt for the pathos of mere silliness, and was indulgent of it. His formality did not arise from party manners, but from tact. He would not take advantage of the vulnerable.

On the following evening, we dined with Harold alone. We spoke of Naples, of friends, books, travels; and of France. Francis thanked Harold for agreeing to write, at F.'s suggestion, an introduction for the forthcoming book of a Neapolitan historian. Harold said that he had accepted with pleasure: "I am always at it with introductions these days. It's the only way I can keep my hand in. As to reading, I shall soon be able to say, with Valéry, *'Je ne lis que les livres dont je fais les préfaces.'*" He mentioned that he now received, from Italian publishers, many new books on Bourbon rule at Naples: "A veritable outpouring." Veritable was one of Harold's words. Francis asked whether, if he were writing his history now, he would be more sympathetic to the Neapolitan revolution of 1799, in the wake of which a generation of the young Neapolitan intelligentsia was brutally destroyed.

Harold: "An enduring tragedy, and obscure to the world." He could not share our belief that the revolution might have succeeded. "Rash," he thought, "and in vain." As to his own view of the event, expressed in his histories: "I was writing in the aftermath of war, and rather had the bit between my teeth against the uniform Leftism proclaimed by Italian intellectuals—a cloak in which many a former fascist sought to cover himself. It was my revulsion against the spectacle of—say, the arch-fascist Malaparte in the arms of the arch-Stalinist Togliatti. And then there was the artistic conformity, all falling into line. Most disheartening." Later, he said, "When I started out, I was greeted as an iconoclast—inaccurately. Now I'm called an anachronism—which I don't mind."

As we were parting that evening, Harold suddenly asked, "Does Graham Greene still come to Capri?" It was a question, one felt, that he had been intending to raise.

We told Harold that Graham was on the island now. "If you can come over, we could lunch together."

Harold, gravely: "I would not care to impose myself on someone who now takes so little pleasure in my society."

We were quiet. Francis said, "What a pity this is."

Harold nodded. "A long association. But his continual air of displeasure has become tiresome."

It was unlike Graham, by then, to have hurt so old a friend.

Harold outlived Graham by three years. On a visit to Florence, late in 1992, we saw him for the last time. He had invited us to lunch. We had been told that he was steadily weakening; and we came up to the house in November light and with the pang of finality—that consciousness, after familiar pleasures, of a leave-taking. Harold, frail, greeted us as ever. I had brought an early, signed copy of his first book of prose, *Cornelian,* to ask for his inscription—"My dear, *puerility,*" he said, taking it up. His signature, that day, at eighty-eight, was unchanged from sixty-four years earlier.

At table, we were six: three elders, with younger companions. I was the only woman. Those three elders—Harold, Francis, and John Pope-Hennessy—have all departed now. During lunch, Harold told me, "I shall never leave Florence again. A time is coming when I may leave this house less and less. I don't mind. I love the house, and never tire of it." He said, "The only regret is for Naples. When I think that I'll never see Naples again, it pains me." A little later, he turned to the others: "We've been speaking of Naples, which I shan't see again." He then raised his head and began to sing.

The song, in dialect, was an old Neapolitan favourite—

> *When the moon comes up at Marechiaro,*
> *Even the fish make love . . .*

He sang it through to the impassioned dying fall at the end. Harold had a fine, firm singing voice and made the song his own; and I have never heard it since without mentally adding, to those old Neapolitan words, the Actonian lilt. The young men serving us came, smiling, from behind their screen to listen; and, when the song was over, added their applause to ours. Harold had again seized the sombre moment and enlivened it.

Following his death, he became for a while something of a target for the strictures of the righteous: a prey of the spectacle, recently renascent, of virtue addressing error. Harold was now a card to play. Ignoring his benefactions and his books, critics derided his affections and pleasures and sifted his ancestry. This, though it might have wounded him, would not, I think, have surprised: throughout his life, some faction or other had sat in judgment over him. If his shade revisits his beloved garden, it certainly does not waste the moonlit evenings there in rancour; but will pass them joyfully, re-experiencing the grand illusion of art in the company of those who count the hours spent with him among the best.

The crisis at Antibes subsided, throbbing. Graham and Yvonne returned to Capri. Although we had, perhaps, some of our best times, these visits could hardly be a resumption. By then, the years and the world gave context only for retrieval amid uncertainties. Graham was paler, older; and that pang of last times might have tinged our evenings together had it not been for his unsubdued argument with life. In his eighties, there was something valiant in the refusal to mellow. He remained fired, as in youth, with engagement and indignation, and by the rightful written word.

In an early essay on Ford Madox Ford, Graham had said that Ford "belonged to the heroic age of English fiction and outlived it." In retrospect, that age seemed to extend a while; and the words can be applied, now, to Graham himself.

At the end of one warm day, we went to drinks at the Rosaio before dinner, driving up between the black ilex of the Anacapri road in one of the island's old, open, ample taxis. Halfway up the winding ascent, there was the climatic change to cool air, and a green smell of vegetation; and, for those who dared look down, the Roman ruins fringing the shore near the port of Augustus. That was, in fact, the last time we went to the Rosaio. From Graham's rooftop terrace, there was the immoderate sunset over Ischia, inflaming white walls, walled garden, coast, sea, and sky: a conflagration that only Graham could have failed to remark on.

We walked to the Rondinella, and were seated at the end of a narrow terrace. The restaurant was soon full, but we were secluded, with only one tiny table nearby. Graham was in good humour, pleased; and we spoke of Henry James.

At the dawn of the twentieth century, Henry James had arrived on Capri. Literarily speaking, it might seem that the island lacked only that. One blue day, he came on a creaking steamer that gradually "drew closer beneath the prodigious island—beautiful, horrible, and haunted." Beautiful, indisputably; haunted, extravagantly; horrible, James tells us, because of its antique emperor and his victims—the literal cliffhanger of the Tiberian years. Perhaps, Francis thought, horrible also in that archaic sense of the word—still valid in Italian—of inspiring awe; as a waterfall or an abyss can be, in Italian, *un orrido.*

Graham was interested in the word, but said, "Something odd has happened to me with Henry James."

No two encounters with Graham were ever the same, he saw to that. But it was a familiar moment—the evening scene of Italian pleasures and trellissed vines, a young man at the nearby table reading his *Corriere,* the lovers passing in pairs in the street just below us; and Graham turning to Henry James.

He told us that, "after a lifetime's enthrallment to James," he found that he could no longer read the late and "greatest" novels—*The Wings of the Dove, The Golden Bowl.* "And now I have the very criticisms I despised as philistine, that the writing is self-indulgent, convoluted, effete; that the story inches along, losing its hold. I've loved those books so long. And now I can't read them."

It might be a mood. "No, no, I can't get back the feeling for them. The stories and the letters remain thrilling, and others of the novels. But I don't suppose I'll read those last books again."

He talked wonderfully of the stories and novellas, mentioning early and obscure tales as well as the great ones. When, of "In the Cage," I said, "It might have been better not to have them meet," Graham asked, "You think that the story would have been greater that way? Yes, perhaps—but quite different." When Francis said that many of James's stories were underlain by communicated terror, Graham smiled with satisfaction: "Yes, strong in much of his work." He spoke of dreams that James had experienced, related, and used. (This interest may have influenced Graham's little, late book of his own dreams.)

The two men talked of "The Jolly Corner," James's unresolved masterpiece of dread and self-revelation. Turning to me, Graham asked, "What do you make of it, 'The Jolly Corner'?"

I said, *"Un orrido."*

It was the moment, things being so agreeable, in which Graham might have turned the tables: he still had his arsenal of spanners to throw into the works. One was aware of this; but the meal went pleasurably to its conclusion, and Graham asked for his bill.

Then, abruptly, with a voice that rang out theatrically: "There's a spy in this restaurant."

People turned, stared. We ourselves were not astonished.

"This young man has been listening. He hasn't turned a page in half an hour. He's been watching us."

Useless to point out—Graham, knowing it was you, understanding English, why not want to hear you speak of Henry James?

The young man got up and left.

Painful.

Graham said, "He may have followed us here." Yet he knew.

The next evening, at Gemma, Francis asked him, "Have you seen anything more of that young man?"

Graham laughed.

That year, after leaving Capri, Yvonne wrote to us enclosing an article promised during the evening at the Rondinella. Referring to their busy return to Antibes, where *"le calme et la tranquillité de*

Capri, eux aussi semblent bien loin," she looked to a reunion in the following year. But, in 1989, Graham wrote: "We were sorry to miss you. The journey from here becomes more and more tiring and we are thinking of selling." He had owned the Rosaio for more than forty years. The house had given him shelter longer than any other.

We stayed in touch by letter and, occasionally, by telephone. Graham's voice grew remote, exhausted, his energies ebbing at last. He was moving, with Yvonne, to an apartment near Geneva, for medical care. In a letter of August 1990, he told us:

> It's very sad to have to sell the Rosaio but the journey was really becoming too much and I have been very ill with anaemia and pneumonia on top of it. I have to have blood transfusions every two weeks and vitamin injections every three days, but I hope in the end I shall get out of this tiresome position. Yvonne and I send our love.

Possibly to temper his sober meaning, he added in a postscript: "Perhaps I'll be able to meet you and Francis one day at some nearer point than Capri."

In New York, on the fourth of April 1991, as we prepared our breakfast, I turned on the radio for the news. The first announcement reported Graham's death on the previous evening. We had expected it. But Francis said, "What a shock it is."

In the previous September, at the death of Alberto Moravia, the Italian newspaper *La Repubblica* had carried across its front page the headline: SENZA MORAVIA—"Without Moravia." As with

Moravia in Italy, there was scarcely a literate person in the English-reading world who had grown up without some consciousness of Graham Greene—of his unquiet, unappeasable spirit and his ability to put clear words to the world's malaise. Almost to the end, he had kept pace with his convulsed century, detached but not dispassionate; aiming for the heart.

Yvonne had shared his later life with unresisting love. Now she wrote to us: *"C'est ce 'plus jamais' que je n'arrive pas à accepter."* Recounting Graham's last hours, she told us of his urgent wish to be allowed to die, that he should not be revived, and did not regret departure—*"au point que ses dernières paroles ont été* 'But I *want* to go,'" as he lapsed into a coma. A few hours earlier, with Yvonne and her daughter at his bedside, he had spoken with acceptance and simplicity of his own death; and Martine had reminded him of the work that would endure. Graham replied that he believed he had written "some good books" and that "I may be remembered, perhaps, from time to time—in the way that one recalls Flaubert." Yvonne wondered if we could shed light on that incongruous remark. It remains an enigma.

In 1994, at Francis's death, Yvonne wrote to recall, with loving-kindness, our evenings *à quatre*—the foursome from which two had departed. "Maybe, now, they have found each other and go on discoursing on Flaubert."

❧

In 1992, following Graham's death, a letter came to me from Michael Richey, with whom, over years, we had lost touch:

I wonder if you remember a Christmas at Capri, so many years ago now, when I was staying with Graham Greene and we first met? As I remember things Graham and I had been to Mass in the Cathedral and were having a coffee in a bar nearby, talking I think about the revised liturgy and the new practice of greeting your neighbour at a particular juncture. Graham thought it a useful way of introducing yourself and quoted a poem but got stuck and you out of the blue . . . picked it up. After that we met several times, at Laetitia Cerio's I think and I am not sure we did not spend new year's eve together. Graham had gone off somewhere . . . It's a pretty story and I'd like to get it right. What was the poem and what the passage?

That was the genesis of this memoir.

In his early decades—in "the years of power"—Graham was close to many writers, none of whom wrote of him at length or intimately, and most of whom are now dead. Through all his adult life, there is scant testimony, other than his own, to suggest what it was to be habitually in his company, to walk with him in a street, to exchange opinions, literature, laughter, and something of one's self; to observe his moods and responses, suffer his temper, and witness his attachments; to see him grow old. It seemed time, too, that a woman should write of Graham Greene.

When friends die, one's own credentials change: one becomes a survivor.

Graham has now had several biographers, one of whom, in creating, over twenty years, the quarry for posterity, has served him mightily. I hope, even so, that there is room for the remembrance of somebody who knew him—not wisely, perhaps, but fairly well—on an island that was "not his kind of place," but where he came season after season, year after year; and where he, too, will be subsumed into the capacious story. These recollections are bound up with glimpses of that place, and with memories of its men and women; above all, with images of two tall men sitting at ease in the café, as years pass, talking of the great writers: living impressions that may stay vivid into the Millennium—or so very little longer.

A c k n o w l e d g e m e n t s

In thanking friends and acquaintances for practical help and kind
encouragement during my work on this memoir, I should like, in
particular, to recall the generosity of the following persons:

Nicholas Scheetz, Norman Sherry, Yvonne Cloetta, Michael
Richey, and Alison and William Parente.

My gratitude also goes to

Lily Aprile Gravino, Anna Maria Boniello, Alice Weber
Cerasaro, Annetta Cinefra, Everett Fahy, Pietro Quirico,
Giuseppina and Riccardo Rocchi, Raffaele and Maria
Vacca, Oliver Walston, and Ausilia Veneruso and Riccardo
Esposito of the Libreria La Conchiglia, Capri—

and to

Lynn Nesbit, my agent and friend
Jonathan Galassi and his colleagues at Farrar, Straus and
    Giroux
Mike Dibb and his team at the BBC
Lennie Goodings, at Virago.

In addition, I thank the executors of the Graham Greene Estate for
permission to quote from letters. And I express my appreciation
for kind loans of photographs and private papers.

SH